SHAMBHALA
CLASSICS

Training the Mind

& CULTIVATING LOVING-KINDNESS

Chögyam Trungpa

EDITED BY JUDITH L. LIEF

SHAMBHALA · *Boston & London* · 2003

SHAMBHALA PUBLICATIONS, INC.
Horticultural Hall
300 Massachusetts Avenue
Boston, Massachusetts 02115
www.shambhala.com

9 8 7 6 5 4 3 2

Printed in the United States of America

∞ This edition is printed on acid-free paper that
meets the American National Standards Institute
z39.48 Standard.

Distributed in the United States by Random House,
Inc., and in Canada by Random House of Canada Ltd

Library of Congress Cataloging-in-Publication Data
Trungpa, Chögyam, 1939–
Training the mind and cultivating loving-kindness/
Chögyam Trungpa, edited by Judith L. Lief.
—1st ed.   p. cm.   Includes index
ISBN 0-87773-954-4
ISBN 1-59030-051-3 (Shambhala Classics)
1. Bodhicitta (Buddhism) 2. Self-control—Religious
aspects—Buddhism. L. Lief, Judith L.   II. Title.
BQ4398.S.178   1993   93-520
294-3′444—dc20   CIP

Contents

• •
•

Contents

Foreword

•
•
•

I AM BOTH HONORED AND DELIGHTED to have been asked to write this preface to the new edition of Chögyam Trungpa Rinpoche's marvelous book about training the mind in the ways of loving-kindness and compassion.

Since 1981 the fifty-nine slogans that are contained in this book have been the primary focus of both my personal practice and of my teaching. For all these years, I have contemplated Trungpa Rinpoche's commentaries on the slogans almost daily, and I can say without exaggerating that they have transformed my life.

The method I have used in this continually deepening exploration is one that Trungpa Rinpoche recommended to his students. Using a set of cards printed with each of the slogans, I shuffle the stack each morning and draw the slogan for the day. Then I read from this book about what Rinpoche has to say, sometimes jotting down notes on the back of the card. This is followed by my best try to live by the meaning of the slogan throughout my day. Sometimes I forget the slogan all day long, only to be reminded of its message when I come back to my room at night. Usually, however, if something challenging arises, the slogan of the day or perhaps a different one altogether will come to mind and provide me with "on the spot" instruction. This always introduces me to a bigger perspective. I begin to have increasing confidence that I can utilize the slogans to be less reactive and to see things more clearly throughout my whole life. Slogan practice indeed continues to help me transform all circumstances into the path of enlightenment. Even the most difficult of situations have become more and more workable. The more I get hooked by what is going on, the more these challenges become a remarkable teacher, one that can open and soften me and make me wiser.

The key is, however, to acknowledge that I am hooked and to work with the slogan, rather than to continue to get all worked up. We are all experts at escalating our emotional reactivity, fanning the fire with habitual thoughts and predictable strategies. For me, the slogan contemplation interrupts this momentum and brings a fresh take into the dynamic. My gratitude to this practice and to my teacher Chögyam Trungpa Rinpoche is limitless. I feel there is no way I could sufficiently repay his kindness in introducing me to these profound yet simple teachings and encouraging me to practice them. As Rinpoche says in his introduction, "You can just follow the book and do as it says, which is extraordinarily powerful and such a relief."

These words certainly resonate with my personal experience, and I am eager that others also give this practice a try. I feel sure that by taking these words to heart many will profit as I have. May you be one of these fortunate ones now and in the future.

—*Pema Chödrön*

Editor's Preface

.· ·.
·

T HIS BOOK IS A TRANSLATION by the Nālandā Translation
Committee of *The Root Text of the Seven Points of Training the
Mind* by Chekawa Yeshe Dorje, with a commentary based on oral
teachings presented by Chögyam Trungpa, Rinpoche. In his teaching on
this subject, Trungpa Rinpoche utilized as a central reference the commentary by Jamgön Kongtrül the Great, entitled in Tibetan *Changchup
Shunglam* (*The Basic Path toward Enlightenment*), which was included
in the collection of the principal teachings of Tibetan Buddhism that the
latter compiled, known as *The Five Treasuries*. (Trungpa Rinpoche's
own teacher, Jamgön Kongtrül of Sechen, was an incarnation of this
leading nineteenth-century teacher.)

The seven points of mind training are attributed to the great Indian
Buddhist teacher Atisha Dipankara Shrijnana, who was born of royal
heritage in Bengal in 982 C.E. Thus, the list of mind training slogans
compiled by Chekawa is often referred to as the Atisha Slogans.
Having renounced palace life as a teenager, Atisha studied and practiced extensively in India and later in Sumatra, with his principal
teacher, Dharmakirti (also known as Serlingpa in Tibetan), from whom
he received the instructions on bodhichitta and mind training. Upon his
return to India, he began to reestablish these once-lost teachings and
took a post at Vikramashila, a famous Buddhist monastic university. Invited to bring the teachings on mind training to Tibet, he taught there
for about thirteen years, until his death in approximately 1054, having
transmitted this body of wisdom to his closest Tibetan disciple,
Dromtönpa, the founder of the Kadam lineage of Tibetan Buddhism.[1]

For some time, the Atisha slogans were kept secret and transmitted only to close disciples. The first to write them down was the Kadampa teacher Lang-ri Thangpa (1054–1123). They became more widely known after they were summarized by Geshe Chekawa Yeshe Dorje (1101–1175) in *The Root Text of the Seven Points of Training the Mind*. Geshe Chekawa encountered many lepers in the course of his teaching and instructed them in mind training. It is said that several of them were thereby cured of their disease. His teachings were thus sometimes referred to by the Tibetans as "the dharma for leprosy." When Chekawa noticed that these teachings even seemed to benefit his unruly brother, who had no interest in the dharma, he decided that it would be appropriate to make them more widely available. Atisha's teachings on mind training are thus now practiced by all the major lineages of Tibetan Buddhism, and have been for centuries.[2]

The Root Text of the Seven Points of Training the Mind is a list of fifty-nine slogans, which form a pithy summary instruction on the view and practical application of mahayana Buddhism. The study and practice of these slogans is a very practical and earthy way of reversing our ego-clinging and of cultivating tenderness and compassion. They provide a method of training our minds through both formal meditation practice and using the events of everyday life as a means of awakening.

This volume is not based on a single seminar, but rather is a compilation of teachings and remarks given over a period of years. The Vidyadhara[3] first presented the mahayana teachings of the Kadampa slogans in 1975, at the third annual Vajradhatu[4] Seminary, one of thirteen three-month advanced teaching programs he taught between 1973 and 1986. In subsequent seminaries he further elaborated upon the theory and practice of mind training.

Mind training, or slogan practice, has two aspects: meditation and postmeditation practice. In Tibetan, the meditation practice is called *tonglen*, or sending and taking, and is based upon the seventh slogan: "Sending and taking should be practiced alternately. / These two should ride the breath." Trungpa Rinpoche introduced the formal meditation practice of tonglen to his students at the 1979 Seminary and he encouraged them to incorporate tonglen into their daily meditation practice. He also encouraged them to work with the postmeditation practice of

joining every aspect of their lives with meditative discipline through the application of the slogans.

In working with his own students, Trungpa Rinpoche placed great emphasis on the practice of formless meditation, the development of mindfulness and awareness, as the foundation. He initially transmitted tonglen practice only to senior students who already had extensive experience in sitting meditation and the study of Buddhist teachings. When the study and practice of mind training are presented in such a context, the danger of interpreting these teachings in a moralistic or conceptual fashion is reduced.

Later the practice of tonglen began to be introduced to students upon the occasion of taking the bodhisattva vow, a formal statement of their aspiration to dedicate their lives to the benefit of others. Over time, tonglen practice was introduced in a variety of contexts. The Naropa University, a Buddhist-inspired university in Boulder, Colorado, includes tonglen training in its clinical psychology program. This training has also been offered as an aspect of the Buddhist-Christian dialogues offered at the Naropa University. Participants in one-month-long meditation intensives, called *dathüns* in Tibetan, are now regularly introduced to tonglen practice, and if they desire more intensive training, they may take part in specialized tonglen dathüns. Tonglen is included in a monthly practice for the sick as well as in Vajradhatu funeral ceremonies.

Through slogan practice, we begin to realize that our habitual tendency, even in our smallest gestures, is one of self-centeredness. That tendency is quite entrenched and affects all of our activities, even our so-called benevolent behavior. The practice of tonglen is a direct reversal of such a habit pattern and is based on the practice of putting others before self. Starting with our friends, and then extending to our acquaintances and eventually even our enemies, we expand our field of awareness to accept others and be of benefit to them. We do this not because we are martyrs or have suppressed our self-concern, but because we have begun to accept ourselves and our world. Slogan practice opens up a greater field of tenderness and strength, so that our actions are based on appreciation rather than the ongoing cycle of hope and fear.

Coming face to face with this most basic contrast of altruism and self-centeredness takes considerable courage and daring. It gets right to

the heart of the spiritual path and allows no room for even the slightest deception or holding back. It is a very basic, nitty-gritty practice.

Tonglen is a particularly powerful way of dealing with pain and loss. In relating to illness or death—our own or another's—tonglen helps us overcome our struggle with and rejection of such experiences and relate more simply and directly.

The formal practice of tonglen, like mindfulness-awareness practice, works with the medium of the breath. In order to begin, it is essential first to ground oneself by means of mindfulness and awareness training. That is the foundation upon which tonglen is based. Tonglen practice itself has three stages. To begin with, you rest your mind briefly, for a second or two, in a state of openness. This stage is somewhat abrupt and has a quality of "flashing" on basic stillness and clarity. Next, you work with texture. You breathe in a feeling of heat, darkness, and heaviness, a sense of claustrophobia, and you breathe out a feeling of coolness, brightness, and lightness—a sense of freshness. You feel these qualities going in and out, through all your pores. Having established the general feeling or tone of tonglen, you begin to work with mental contents. Whatever arises in your experience, you simply breathe in what is not desirable and breathe out what is desirable. Starting with your immediate experience, you expand that to include people around you and other sentient beings who are suffering in the same way as you. For instance, if you are feeling inadequate, you begin by breathing that in and breathing out your personal sense of competence and adequacy. Then you extend the practice, broadening it beyond your personal concerns to connect with the poignancy of those feelings in your immediate surroundings and throughout the world. The essential quality of this practice is one of opening your heart— wholeheartedly taking in and wholeheartedly letting go. In tonglen nothing is rejected: whatever arises is further fuel for the practice.

Trungpa Rinpoche stressed the importance of the oral tradition, in which practices are transmitted personally and directly from teacher to student. In that way students participate directly in an unbroken wisdom tradition, going back many generations to the time of the Buddha himself. The essential living quality of practice being conveyed is a very human one and cannot be acquired simply from books. Therefore, it is recommended that before embarking on the formal practice of sending

and taking, if at all possible, one should meet with an experienced practitioner to discuss the practice and receive formal instruction.

The postmeditation practice is based upon the spontaneous recall of appropriate slogans in the thick of daily life. Rather than making a heavy-handed or deliberate effort to guide your actions in accordance with the slogans, a quality of spontaneous reminder is evoked through the study of these traditional aphorisms. If you study these seven points of mind training and memorize the slogans, you will find that they arise effortlessly in your mind at the oddest times. They have a haunting quality, and in their recurrence they can lead you gradually to a more and more subtle understanding of the nature of kindness and compassion.

The slogans have a way of continually turning in on themselves, so that any attempt to rely on these sayings as crutches to support a particular moral view is undermined. The approach to moral action here is one of removing obstacles of limited vision, fear and self-clinging, so that one's actions are not burdened by the weight of self-concern, projections, and expectations. The slogans are meant to be "practiced." That is, they need to be studied and memorized. At the same time, they need to be "let go." They are merely conceptual tools pointing to nonconceptual realization.

As is usual in Buddhist teachings, there is an element of playfulness and irony in the way one slogan often undermines its predecessor and thereby enlarges one's view. They form a loop in which nothing is excluded. Whatever arises in one's mind or experience is let go into the greater space of awareness that slogan practice generates. It is this openness of mind that becomes the basis for the cultivation of compassion.

The view of morality presented through the Kadampa slogans is similar to that of Shakespeare's famous lines, "The quality of mercy is not strained, it falleth as the gentle rain from heaven." There is no notion of moral battlefield in which we ward off evil and fight for the right. The traditional Buddhist image for compassion is that of the sun, which shines beneficently and equally on all. It is the sun's nature to shine; there is no struggle. Likewise, compassion is a natural human activity, once the veils and obstacles to its expression are removed.

The Vidyadhara encouraged his students to include tonglen in their daily meditation practice and to memorize the slogans. He would have individual slogans beautifully calligraphed and posted at Vajradhatu seminaries. You never knew when you might come across one. For instance, you might find "Be grateful to everyone" posted in the kitchen, or "Drive all blames into one" hanging from a tree. The slogans are meant to be contemplated—one by one. For that reason the Vidyadhara encouraged students to use printed slogan cards as daily reminders and provocateurs.*

In their earthiness and simplicity, may these teachings inspire us to cultivate kindness and compassion, and not to give up on ourselves or others. May they provoke fearlessness in overcoming the tenacious grip of ego. May they enable us to put into practice our most heartfelt aspirations to benefit all sentient beings on the path of awakening.

*For information on obtaining slogan cards, see page 127.

Acknowledgments

• •
•

W ORK ON THIS BOOK BEGAN many years ago and involved the efforts of many people. Members of the Nālandā Translation Committee worked closely with the Vidyadhara, Chögyam Trungpa, Rinpoche, on an initial translation of the Kadampa slogans in 1981 and a subsequent revision in 1986. Translators involved at that time included Lama Ugyen Shenpen, Sherab Chödzin, Dorje Loppön Lodrö Dorje, Robin Kornman, Larry Mermelstein, and Scott Wellenbach. In preparation for this volume, the Translation Committee carefully reviewed its work on this text again, which resulted in some further revisions included here. Committee members involved with this latest revision include Lama Ugyen Shenpen, Jules Levinson, Larry Mermelstein, Mark Nowakowski, John Rockwell, and Scott Wellenbach. At the same time, a translation was prepared of "Forty-six Ways in Which a Bodhisattva Fails."

Sarah Coleman of the Vajradhatu Editorial Department worked on the original manuscript and was also present at the initial translation meetings with the Vidyadhara. She later held a series of meetings with the Vidyadhara to clarify and refine the commentary. Tingdzin Ötro of Gampo Abbey did a fastidious job of compiling on computer the Vidyadhara's teaching on the practice of the Kadampa slogans, which was scattered throughout many years of Vajradhatu Seminary Transcripts. In addition, the recording, transcribing, and preservation of Trungpa Rinpoche's teachings has taken the work of countless Vajradhatu Archive volunteers, to whom I am most grateful.

Ken McLeod's pioneering translation of Jamgön Kongtrül's commentary on mind training, given him by Venerable Kalu Rinpoche and

Acknowledgments

first published in 1974, *The Great Path of Awakening* (Shambhala, 1987), has been a continuing resource for students and of great help in the preparation of this manuscript.

I would like to thank Mrs. Diana Mukpo, who has provided ongoing support for the Dharma Ocean Series and given her permission and encouragement to publish these teachings.

Most especially, I would like to thank the Vidyadhara, Venerable Chögyam Trungpa, Rinpoche, who showed us a pragmatic way of cultivating kindness and who was persistent in encouraging us to make these teachings available for the benefit of beings in these difficult times.

—*Judith L. Lief*

Training the Mind
& CULTIVATING LOVING-KINDNESS

Introduction

.: .

IN THE MAHAYANA TRADITION[1] we experience a sense of gentleness toward ourselves, and a sense of friendliness to others begins
to arise. That friendliness or compassion is known in Tibetan as *nyingje*,
which literally means "noble heart." We are willing to commit ourselves
to working with all sentient beings. But before we actually launch into
that project, we first need a lot of training.

The obstacle to becoming a mahayanist is not having enough sympathy for others and for oneself—that is the basic point. And that problem can be dealt with by practical training, which is known as *lojong*
practice, "training the mind." That training gives us a path, a way to
work with our crude and literal and raw and rugged styles, a way to become good mahayanists. Ignorant or stupid students of the mahayana
sometimes think that they have to glorify themselves; they want to become leaders or guides. We have a technique or practice for overcoming that problem. That practice is the development of humility, which
is connected with training the mind.

The basic mahayana vision is to work for the benefit of others and
create a situation that will benefit others. Therefore, you take the attitude that you are willing to dedicate yourself to others. When you take
that attitude, you begin to realize that others are more important than
yourself. Because of that vision of mahayana, because you adopt that
attitude, and because you actually find that others are more important—with all three of those together, you develop the mahayana practice of training the mind.

Hinayana discipline is fundamentally one of *taming* the mind. By

I

working with the various forms of unmindfulness, we begin to become thorough and precise, and our discipline becomes good. When we are thoroughly tamed by the practice of *shamatha* discipline, or mindfulness practice, as well as trained by *vipashyana*, or awareness, in how to hear the teachings, we begin to develop a complete understanding of the dharma. After that, we also begin to develop a complete understanding of how, in our particular state of being tamed, we can relate with others.

In the mahayana we talk more in terms of *training* the mind. That is the next step. The mind is already tamed, therefore it can be trained. In other words, we have been able to domesticate our mind by practicing hinayana discipline according to the principles of the buddhadharma. Having domesticated our mind, then we can use it further. It's like the story of capturing a wild cow in the old days. Having captured the wild cow, having domesticated it, you find that the cow becomes completely willing to relate with its tamers. In fact, the cow likes being domesticated. So at this point the cow is part of our household. Once upon a time it wasn't that way—I'm sure cows were wild and ferocious before we domesticated them.

Training the mind is known as *lojong* in Tibetan: *lo* means "intelligence," "mind," "that which can perceive things"; *jong* means "training" or "processing." The teachings of lojong consist of several steps or points of mahayana discipline. The basic discipline of mind training or lojong is a sevenfold cleaning or processing of one's mind.

This book is based on the basic Kadampa text, *The Root Text of the Seven Points of Training the Mind*, and on the commentary by Jamgön Kongtrül. In Tibetan the commentary is called *Changchup Shunglam*. *Shung* is the word used for "government" and also for "main body." So *shung* means "main governing body." For instance, we could call the Tibetan government *pö shung*—*pö* meaning "Tibet," *shung* meaning "government." The government that is supposed to run a country is a wide administration rather than a narrow administration: it takes care of the psychology of the country, the economics, politics, and domestic situations. *Shung* is actually the working basis, the main working stream. *Lam* means "path." So *shunglam* is a general highway, so to speak, a basic process of working toward enlightenment. In other words, it is the mahayana approach. It is the highway that everybody goes on, a wide way, extraordinarily wide and extraordinarily open. *Changchup* means "enlightenment," *shung* means "wide" or "basic," and *lam* means "path." So the title of the commentary is *The Basic Path Toward Enlightenment.*

The main text is based on Atisha's teachings on lojong and comes from the Kadam school of Tibetan Buddhism, which developed around the time of Marpa and Milarepa, when Tibetan monasticism had begun to take place and become deep-rooted. The Kagyüpas received these instructions on the proper practice of mahayana Buddhism through Gampopa, who studied with Milarepa as well as with Kadam teachers. There is what is known as the contemplative Kadam school and the intellectual Kadam school. What we are doing here is related to the Kadam school's contemplative tradition. The Gelukpas specialized in dialectics and took a more philosophical approach to understanding the Kadam tradition.

The word *kadam* has an interesting meaning for us. *Ka* means "command," as when a general gives a pep talk to his or her troops or a king gives a command to his ministers. Or we could say "Logos," or "Word," as in the Christian tradition: "In the beginning was the Word." That kind of Word is a fundamental sacred command, the first that was uttered at all! In this case, *ka* refers to a sense of absolute truth and a sense of practicality or workability from the individual's point of view. *Dam* is "oral teaching," "personal teaching," that is, a manual on how to handle our life properly. So *ka* and *dam* mixed together means that all the *ka*, all the commands or messages, are regarded as practical and workable oral teachings. They are regarded as a practical working basis for students who are involved with contemplative and meditative disciplines. That is the basic meaning of *kadam*.

The few lists presented here are very simple ones, nothing particularly philosophical. It is purely what one of the great Kagyü teachers regarded as a "grandmother's fingerpoint." When a grandmother says, "This is the place where I used to go and pick corn, collect wild vegetables," she usually uses her finger rather than writing on paper or using a map. So it is a grandmother's approach at this point.

In my own case, having studied philosophy a lot, the first time Jamgön Kongtrül suggested that I read and study this book, *Changchup Shunglam*, I was relieved that Buddhism was so simple and that you could actually do something about it. You can actually practice. You can just follow the book and do as it says, which is extraordinarily powerful and such a relief. And that sense of simplicity still continues. It is so precious and so direct. I do not know what kind of words to use to describe it. It is somewhat rugged, but at the same time it is so soothing to read such writing. That is one of the characteristics of Jamgön Kongtrül—he can change his tone completely, as if he were a different author altogether. Whenever he writes on a particular subject, he changes his approach accordingly, and his basic awareness to relate with the audience becomes entirely different.

Jamgön Kongtrül's commentary on the Kadampa slogans is one of the best books I studied in the early stages of my monastic kick. I was going to become a simple little monk. I was going to study these things and become a good little Buddhist and a contemplative-type person. Such a thread still holds throughout my life. In spite of complications in my life and organizational problems, I still feel that I am basically a simple, romantic Buddhist who has immense feeling toward the teachers and the teaching.

What has been said is a drop of golden liquid. Each time you read such a book it confirms again and again that there is something about it which makes everything very simple and direct. That makes me immensely happy. I sleep well, too. There is a hard-edged quality of cutting down preconceptions and other ego battles that might be involved in presenting the teaching. But at the same time there is always a soft spot of devotion and simplicity in mahayana Buddhism which you can never forget. That is very important. I am not particularly trying to be dramatic. If it comes through that way, it's too bad. But I really do feel extraordinarily positive about Jamgön Kongtrül and his approach to this teaching.

POINT ONE

The Preliminaries,
Which Are a Basis
for Dharma Practice

I

First, train in the preliminaries.

In practicing the slogans and in your daily life, you should maintain an
awareness of [1] the preciousness of human life and the particular good
fortune of life in an environment in which you can hear the teachings
of buddhadharma; [2] the reality of death, that it comes suddenly and
without warning; [3] the entrapment of karma—that whatever you do,
whether virtuous or not, only further entraps you in the chain of cause
and effect; and [4] the intensity and inevitability of suffering for yourself and for all sentient beings. This is called "taking an attitude of the
four reminders."

With that attitude as a base, you should call upon your guru with
devotion, inviting into your self the atmosphere of sanity inspired by his
or her example, and vowing to cut the roots of further ignorance and
suffering. This ties in very closely with the notion of *maitri*, or loving-
kindness. In the traditional analogy of one's spiritual path, the only pure
loving object seems to be somebody who can show you the path. You

could have a loving relationship with your parents, relatives, and so forth, but there are still problems with that: your neurosis goes along with it. A pure love affair can only take place with one's teacher. So that ideal sympathetic object is used as a starting point, a way of developing a relationship beyond your own neurosis. Particularly in the mahayana, you relate to the teacher as someone who cheers you up from depression and brings you down from excitement, a kind of moderator principle. The teacher is regarded as important from that point of view.

This slogan establishes the contrast between samsara—the epitome of pain, imprisonment, and insanity—and the root guru—the embodiment of openness, freedom, and sanity—as the fundamental basis for all practice. As such, it is heavily influenced by the vajrayana tradition.

POINT TWO

The Main Practice, Which Is Training in Bodhichitta

ULTIMATE AND RELATIVE BODHICHITTA

Ultimate Bodhichitta and the Paramita of Generosity

The ultimate or absolute bodhichitta principle is based on developing the paramita of generosity, which is symbolized by a wish-fulfilling jewel. The Tibetan word for generosity, *jinpa*, means "giving," "opening," or "parting." So the notion of generosity means not holding back but giving constantly. Generosity is self-existing openness, complete openness. You are no longer subject to cultivating your own scheme or project. And the best way to open yourself up is to make friends with yourself and with others.

Traditionally, there are three types of generosity. The first one is ordinary generosity, giving material goods or providing comfortable situations for others. The second one is the gift of fearlessness. You reassure others and teach them that they don't have to feel completely tormented and freaked out about their existence. You help them to see that there is basic goodness and spiritual practice, that there is a way for them to sustain their lives. That is the gift of fearlessness. The third type of generosity is the gift of dharma. You show others that there is a path that consists of discipline, meditation, and intellect or knowledge. Through all three types of generosity, you can open up other people's minds. In that way their closedness, wretchedness, and small thinking can be turned into a larger vision.

That is the basic vision of mahayana altogether: to let people think bigger, think greater. We can afford to open ourselves and join the rest of the world with a sense of tremendous generosity, tremendous goodness, and tremendous richness. The more we give, the more we gain—although what we might gain should not particularly be our reason for giving. Rather, the more we give, the more we are inspired to give constantly. And the gaining process happens naturally, automatically, always.

The opposite of generosity is stinginess, holding back—having a poverty mentality, basically speaking. The basic principle of the ultimate bodhichitta slogans is to rest in the eighth consciousness, or *alaya*, and not follow our discursive thoughts. *Alaya* is a Sanskrit word meaning "basis," or sometimes "abode" or "home," as in *Himalaya*, "abode of snow." So it has that idea of a vast range. It is the fundamental state of consciousness, before it is divided into "I" and "other," or into the various emotions. It is the basic ground where things are processed, where things exist. In order to rest in the nature of alaya, you need to go beyond your poverty attitude and realize that your alaya is as good as anybody else's alaya. You have a sense of richness and self-sufficiency. You can do it, and you can afford to give out as well. And the ultimate bodhichitta slogans [slogans 2–6] are the basic points of reference through which we are going to familiarize ourselves with ultimate bodhichitta.

Ultimate bodhichitta is similar to the absolute *shunyata* principle. And whenever there is the absolute shunyata principle, we have to have a basic understanding of absolute compassion at the same time. *Shunyata* literally means "openness" or "emptiness." Shunyata is basically understanding nonexistence. When you begin realizing nonexistence, then you can afford to be more compassionate, more giving. A problem is that usually we would like to hold on to our territory and fixate on that particular ground. Once we begin to fixate on that ground, we have no way to give. Understanding shunyata means that we begin to realize that there is no ground to get, that we are ultimately free, nonaggressive, open. We realize that we are actually nonexistent ourselves. We are not—*no*, rather.[1] Then we can give. We have lots to gain and nothing to lose at that point. It is very basic.

Compassion is based on some sense of "soft spot" in us. It is as if we had a pimple on our body that was very sore—so sore that we do not want to rub it or scratch it. During our shower we do not want to rub too much soap over it because it hurts. There is a sore point or soft spot which happens to be painful to rub, painful to put hot or cold water over.

That sore spot on our body is an analogy for compassion. Why? Because even in the midst of immense aggression, insensitivity in our life, or laziness, we always have a soft spot, some point we can cultivate—or at least not bruise. Every human being has that kind of basic sore spot, including animals. Whether we are crazy, dull, aggressive, ego-tripping, whatever we might be, there is still that sore spot taking place in us. An open wound, which might be a more vivid analogy, is always there. That open wound is usually very inconvenient and problematic. We don't like it. We would like to be tough. We would like to fight, to come out strong, so we do not have to defend any aspect of ourselves. We would like to attack our enemy on the spot, single-handedly. We would like to lay our trips on everybody completely and properly, so that we have nothing to hide. That way, if somebody decides to hit us back, we are not wounded. And hopefully, nobody will hit us on that sore spot, that wound that exists in us. Our basic makeup, the basic constituents of our mind, are based on passion and compassion at the same time. But however confused we might be, however much of a cosmic monster we might be, still there is an open wound or sore spot in us always. There always will be a sore spot.

Sometimes people translate that sore spot or open wound as "religious conviction" or "mystical experience." But let us give that up. It has nothing to do with Buddhism, nothing to do with Christianity, and moreover, nothing to do with anything else at all. It is just an open wound, a very simple open wound. That is very nice—at least we are accessible somewhere. We are not completely covered with a suit of armor all the time. We have a sore spot somewhere, some open wound somewhere. Such a relief! Thank earth!

Because of that particular sore spot, even if we are a cosmic monster—Mussolini, Mao Tse-tung, or Hitler—we can still fall in love. We can still appreciate beauty, art, poetry, or music. The rest of us could be covered with iron cast shields, but some sore spot always exists in us, which is fantastic. That sore spot is known as embryonic compassion, potential compassion. At least we have some kind of gap, some discrepancy in our state of being which allows basic sanity to shine through.

Our level of sanity could be very primitive. Our sore spot could be just purely the love of tortillas or the love of curries. But that's good enough. We have some kind of opening. It doesn't matter what it is love *of* as long as there is a sore spot, an open wound. That's good. That is where all the germs could get in and begin to impregnate and take possession of us and influence our system. And that is precisely how the compassionate attitude supposedly takes place.

Not only that, but there is also an inner wound, which is called *tathagatagarbha*, or buddha nature. Tathagatagarbha is like a heart that is sliced and bruised by wisdom and compassion. When the external wound and the internal wound begin to meet and to communicate, then we begin to realize that our whole being is made out of one complete sore spot altogether, which is called "bodhisattva fever." That vulnerability is compassion. We really have no way to defend ourselves anymore at all. A gigantic cosmic wound is all over the place—an inward wound and an external wound at the same time. Both are sensitive to cold air, hot air, and little disturbances of atmosphere which begin to affect us both inwardly and outwardly. It is the living flame of love, if you would like to call it that. But we should be very careful what we say about love. What is love? Do we know love? It is a vague word. In this case we are not even calling it love. Nobody before puberty would have any sense of sexuality or of love affairs. Likewise, since we haven't broken through to understand what our soft spot is all about, we cannot talk about love, we can only talk about passion. It might sound too grandiose to talk about compassion. It sounds fantastic, but it actually doesn't say as much as love, which is very heavy. Compassion is a kind of passion, com-passion, which is easy to work with.

There is a slit in our skin, a wound. It's very harsh treatment, in some sense; but on the other hand, it's very gentle. The intention is gentle, but the practice is very harsh. By combining the intention and the practice, you are being "harshed," and also you are being "gentled," so to speak—both together. That makes you into a bodhisattva. You have to go through that kind process. You have to jump into the blender. It is necessary for you to do that. Just jump into the blender and work with it. Then you will begin to feel that you are swimming in the blender. You might even enjoy it a little bit, after you have been processed. So an actual understanding of ultimate bodhichitta only comes from compassion. In other words, a purely logical, professional, or scientific conclusion doesn't bring you to that. The five ultimate bodhichitta slogans are steps toward a compassionate approach.

A lot of you seemingly, very shockingly, are not particularly compassionate. You are not saving your grandma from drowning and you are not saving your pet dog from getting killed. Therefore, we have to go through this subject of compassion. Compassion is a very, very large subject, an extraordinarily large subject, which includes how to *be* compassionate. And actually, ultimate bodhichitta is preparation for relative bodhichitta. Before we cultivate compassion, we first need to understand how to *be* properly. How to love your grandma and how to love your flea or your mosquito—that comes later. The relative aspect of compassion comes much later. If we do not have an understanding of ultimate bodhichitta, then we do not have any understanding of the actual working basis of being compassionate and kind to somebody. We might just join the Red Cross and make nuisances of ourselves and create further garbage.

According to the mahayana tradition, we are told that we can actually arouse twofold bodhichitta: relative bodhichitta and ultimate bodhichitta. We could arouse both of them. Then, having aroused bodhichitta, we can continue further and practice according to the bodhisattva's example. We can be active bodhisattvas.

In order to arouse absolute or ultimate bodhichitta, we have to join shamatha and vipashyana together. Having developed the basic precision of shamatha and the total awareness of vipashyana, we put them together so that they cover the whole of our existence—our behavior patterns and our daily life—everything. In that way, in both meditation and postmeditation practice, mindfulness and awareness are happening simultaneously, all the time. Whether we are sleeping or awake, eating or wandering, precision and awareness are taking place all the time. That is quite a delightful experience.

Beyond that delight, we also tend to develop a sense of friendliness to everythings The early level of irritation and aggression has been processed through, so to speak, by mindfulness and awareness. There is instead a notion of basic goodness, which is described in the Kadam texts as the natural virtue of alaya. This is an important point for us to understand. Alaya is the fundamental state of existence, or consciousness, before it is divided into "I" and "other," or into the various emotions. It is the basic ground where things are processed, where things exist. And its basic state, or natural style, is goodness. It is very benevolent. There is a basic state of existence that is fundamentally good and that we can rely on. There is room to relax, room to open ourselves up. We can make friends with ourselves and with others. That is fundamental virtue or basic goodness, and it is the basis of the possibility of absolute bodhichitta.

Once we have been inspired by the precision of shamatha and the wakefulness of vipashyana, we find that there is room, which gives us the possibility of total naiveté, in the positive sense. The Tibetan for naiveté is *pak-yang*, which means "carefree" or "let loose." We can be carefree with our basic goodness. We do not have to scrutinize or investigate wholeheartedly to make sure that there are no mosquitoes or eggs inside our alaya. The basic goodness of alaya can be cultivated and connected with quite naturally and freely, in a pak-yang way. We can develop a sense of relaxation and release from torment—from this-and-that altogether.

Relative Bodhichitta and the Paramita of Discipline

That brings us to the next stage. Again, instead of remaining at a theoretical, conceptual level alone, we return to the most practical level. In the mahayana our main concern is how to awaken ourselves. We begin to realize that we are not as dangerous as we had thought. We develop some notion of kindness, or maitri, and having developed maitri we begin to switch into *karuna*, or compassion.

The development of relative bodhichitta is connected with the paramita of discipline. It has been said that if you don't have discipline, it is like trying to walk without any legs. You cannot attain liberation without discipline. Discipline in Tibetan is *tsültrim*: *tsül* means "proper," and *trim* means "discipline" or "obeying the rules," literally speaking. So trim could be translated as "rule" or "justice." The basic notion of *tsültrim* goes beyond giving alone; it means having good conduct. It also means having some sense of passionlessness and nonterritoriality. All of that is very much connected with relative bodhichitta.

Relative bodhichitta comes from the simple and basic experience of realizing that you could have a tender heart in any situation. Even the most vicious animals have a tender heart in taking care of their young, or for that matter, in taking care of themselves. From our basic training in shamatha-vipashyana, we begin to realize our basic goodness and to let go with that. We begin to rest in the nature of alaya—not caring and being very naive and ordinary, casual, in some sense. When we let ourselves go, we begin to have a feeling of good existence in ourselves. That could be regarded as the very ordinary and trivial concept of having a good time. Nonetheless, when we have good intentions toward ourselves, it is not because we are trying to achieve anything—we are just trying to be ourselves. As they say, we could come as we are. At that point we have a natural sense that we can afford to give ourselves freedom. We can afford to relax. We can afford to treat ourselves better, trust ourselves more, and let ourselves feel good. The basic goodness of alaya is always there. It is that sense of healthiness and cheerfulness and naiveté that brings us to the realization of relative bodhichitta.

Relative bodhichitta is related with how we start to learn to love each other and ourselves. That seems to be the basic point. It's very difficult for us to learn to love. It would be possible for us to love if an object of fascination were presented to us or if there were some kind of dream or promise presented. Maybe then we could learn to love. But it is very hard for us to learn to love if it means purely giving love without expecting anything in return. It is very difficult to do that. When we decide to love somebody, we usually expect that person to fulfill our desires and conform to our hero worship. If our expectations can be fulfilled, we can fall in love, ideally. So in most of our love affairs, what usually happens is that our love is absolutely conditional. It is more of a business deal than actual love. We have no idea how to communicate a sense of warmth. When we do begin to communicate a sense of warmth to somebody, it makes us very uptight. And when our object of love tries to cheer us up, it becomes an insult.

That is a very aggression-oriented approach. In the mahayana, particularly in the contemplative tradition, love and affection are largely based on free love, open love which does not ask anything in return. It is a mutual dance. Even if during the dance you step on each other's toes, it is not regarded as problematic or an insult. We do not have to get on our high horse or be touchy about that. To learn to love, to learn to open, is one of the hardest things of all for us. Yet we are conditioned by passion all the time. Since we are in the human realm, our main focus or characteristic is passion and lust, all the time. So what the mahayana teachings are based on is the idea of communication, openness, and being without expectations.

When we begin to realize that the nature of phenomena is free from concept, empty by itself, that the chairs and tables and rugs and curtains and walls are no longer in the way, then we can expand our notion of love infinitely. There is nothing in the way. The very purpose of discussing the nature of shunyata is to provide us that emptiness, so that we could fill the whole of space with a sense of affection—love without expectation, without demand, without possession. That is one of the most powerful things that the mahayana has to contribute.

In contrast, hinayana practitioners are very keen on the path of individual salvation, not causing harm to others. They are reasonable and good-thinking and very polite people. But how can you be really polite and keep smiling twenty-four hours a day on the basis of individual salvation alone, without doing anything for others? You are doing everything for yourself all the time, even if you are being kind and nice and polite. That's very hard to do. At the mahayana level, the sense of affection and love has a lot of room—immense room, openness, and daring. There is no time to come out clean, particularly, as long as you generate affection.

The relationship between a mother and child is the foremost analogy used in developing relative bodhichitta practice. According to the medieval Indian and Tibetan traditions, the traditional way of cultivating relative bodhichitta is to choose your mother as the first example of someone you feel soft toward. Traditionally, you feel warm and kindly toward your mother. In modern society, there might be a problem with that. However, you could go back to the medieval idea of the mother principle. You could appreciate her way of sacrificing her own comfort for you. You could remember how she used to wake up in the middle of the night if you cried, how she used to feed you and change your diapers, and all the rest of it. You could remember how you acted as the ruler in your little household, how your mother became your slave. Whenever you cried, she would jump up whether she liked it or not in order to see what was going on with you. Your mother actually did that. And when you were older, she was very concerned about your security and your education and so forth. So in order to develop relative bodhichitta, relative wakeful gentleness, we use our mother as an example, as our pilot light, so to speak. We think about her and realize how much she sacrificed for us. Her kindness is the perfect example of making others more important than yourself.

Reflecting on your own mother is the preliminary to relative bodhichitta practice. You should regard that as your starting point. You might be a completely angry person and have a grudge against the entire universe. You might be a completely frustrated person. But you could still reflect back on your childhood and think of how nice your mother was to you. You could think of that, in spite of your aggression and your resentment. You could remember that there was a time when somebody sacrificed her life for your life, and brought you up to be the person you are now.

The idea of relative bodhichitta in this case is very primitive, in some sense. On the other hand, it is also very enlightening, as bodhichitta should be. Although you might be a completely angry person, you cannot say that in your entire life nobody helped you. Somebody has been kind to you and sacrificed himself or herself for you. Otherwise, if somebody hadn't brought you up, you wouldn't be here as an adult. You could realize that it wasn't just out of obligation but out of her genuineness that your mother brought you up and took care of you when you were helpless. And because of that you are here. That kind of compassion is very literal and very straightforward.

With that understanding, we can begin to extend our sense of nonaggression and nonfrustration and nonanger and nonresentment beyond simply appreciating our mother. This is connected with the paramita of discipline, which is free from passion and has to do with giving in. Traditionally, we use our mother as an example, and then we extend beyond that to our friends and to other people generally. Finally, we even try to feel better toward our enemies, toward people we don't like. So we try to extend that sense of gentleness, softness, and gratitude. We are not particularly talking about the Christian concept of charity, we are talking about how to make ourselves soft and reasonable. We are talking about how we can experience a sense of gratitude toward anybody at all, starting with our mother and going beyond that to include our father as well—and so forth until we include the rest of the world. So in the end we can begin to feel sympathy even toward our bedbugs and mosquitoes.

The starting point of relative bodhichitta practice is realizing that others could actually be more important than ourselves. Other people might provide us with constant problems, but we could still be kind to them. According to the logic of relative bodhichitta, we should feel that we are less important and others are more important—*any* others are more important! Doing so, we begin to feel as though a tremendous burden has been taken off our shoulders. Finally, we realize that there is room to give love and affection elsewhere, to more than just this thing called "me" all the time. "I am this, I am that, I am hungry, I am tired, I am blah-blah-blah." We could consider others. From that point of view, the relative bodhichitta principle is quite simple and ordinary. We could take care of others. We could actually be patient enough to develop selfless service to others. And the relative bodhichitta slogans [slogans 7–10] are directions as to how to develop relative bodhichitta in a very simple manner, a grandmother's approach to reality, so to speak.

ULTIMATE BODHICHITTA SLOGANS

2

Regard all dharmas as dreams.

This slogan is an expression of compassion and openness. It means that whatever you experience in your life—pain, pleasure, happiness, sadness, grossness, refinement, sophistication, crudeness, heat, cold, or whatever—is purely memory. The actual discipline or practice of the bodhisattva tradition is to regard whatever occurs as a phantom. Nothing ever happens. But because nothing happens, everything happens. When we want to be entertained, nothing seems to happen. But in this case, although everything is just a thought in your mind, a lot of underlying percolation takes place. That "nothing happening" is the experience of openness, and that percolation is the experience of compassion.

You can experience that dreamlike quality by relating with sitting meditation practice. When you are reflecting on your breath, suddenly discursive thoughts begin to arise: you begin to see things, to hear things, and to feel things. But all those perceptions are none other than your own mental creation. In the same way, you can see that your hate for your enemy, your love for your friends, and your attitudes toward money, food, and wealth are all a part of discursive thought.

Regarding things as dreams does not mean that you become fuzzy and woolly, that everything has an edge of sleepiness about it. You might actually have a good dream, vivid and graphic. Regarding dharmas as dreams means that although you might think that things are very solid, the way you perceive them is soft and dreamlike. For instance, if you have participated in group meditation practice, your memory of your meditation cushion and the person who sat in front of you is very vivid, as is your memory of your food and the sound of the gong and the bed that you sleep in. But none of those situations is regarded as completely invincible and solid and tough. Everything is shifty.

Things have a dreamlike quality. But at the same time the production of your mind is quite vivid. If you didn't have a mind, you wouldn't be able to perceive anything at all. Because you have a mind, you perceive things. Therefore, what you perceive is a product of your mind, using your sense organs as channels for the sense perceptions.

3

Examine the nature of unborn awareness.

Look at your basic mind, just simple awareness which is not divided into sections, the thinking process that exists within you. Just look at that, see that. Examining does not mean analyzing. It is just viewing things as they are, in the ordinary sense.

The reason our mind is known as *unborn* awareness is that we have no idea of its history. We have no idea where this mind, our crazy mind, began in the beginning. It has no shape, no color, no particular portrait or characteristics. It usually flickers on and off, off and on, all the time. Sometimes it is hibernating; sometimes it is all over the place. Look at your mind. That is a part of ultimate bodhichitta training or discipline. Our mind fluctuates constantly, back and forth, forth and back. Look at that, just *look at that!*

You could get caught up in the fascination of regarding all dharmas as dreams and perpetuate unnecessary visions and fantasies of all kinds. Therefore it is very important to get to this next slogan, "Examine the nature of unborn awareness." When you look beyond the perceptual level alone, when you look at your own mind (which you cannot actually do, but you pretend to do), you find that there is nothing there. You begin to realize that there is nothing to hold on to. Mind is *unborn.* But at the same time, it is *awareness,* because you still perceive things. There is awareness and clarity. Therefore, you should contemplate that by seeing *who* is actually perceiving dharmas as dreams.

If you look further and further, at your mind's root, its base, you will find that it has no color and no shape. Your mind is, basically speaking, somewhat blank. There is nothing to it. We are beginning to cultivate a kind of shunyata possibility; although in this case that possibility is quite primitive, in the sense of simplicity and workability. When we look at the root, when we try to find out why we see things, why we hear sounds, why we feel, and why we smell—if we look beyond that and beyond that—we find a kind of blankness.

That blankness is connected with mindfulness. To begin with, you are mindful of some *thing*: you are mindful of yourself, you are mindful of your atmosphere, and you are mindful of your breath. But if you look at *why* you are mindful, beyond *what* you are mindful of, you begin to find that there is no root. Everything begins to dissolve. That is the idea of examining the nature of unborn awareness.

4
Self-liberate even the antidote.

Looking at our basic mind, we begin to develop a twist of logic. We say, "Well, if nothing has any root, why bother? What's the point of doing this at all? Why don't we just believe that there is no root behind the whole thing?" At that point the next slogan, "Self-liberate even the antidote," is very helpful. The antidote is the realization that our discursive thoughts have no origin. That realization helps a lot; it becomes an antidote or a helpful suggestion. But we need to go beyond that antidote. We should not hang on to the so-whatness of it, the naiveté of it.

The idea of antidote is that everything is empty, so you have nothing to care about. You have an occasional glimpse in your mind that nothing is existent. And because of the nature of that shunyata experience, whether anything great or small comes up, nothing really matters very much. It is like a backslapping joke in which everything is going to be hoo-ha, yuk-yuk-yuk. Nothing is going to matter very much, so let it go. All is shunyata, so who cares? You can murder, you can meditate, you can perform art, you can do all kinds of things—everything is meditation, whatever you do. But there is something very tricky about the whole approach. That dwelling on emptiness is a misinterpretation, called the "poison of shunyata."

Some people say that they do not have to sit and meditate, because they always "understood." But that is very tricky. I have been trying very hard to fight such people. I never trust them at all—unless they actually sit and practice. You cannot split hairs by saying that you might be fishing in a Rocky Mountain spring and still meditating away; you might be driving your Porsche and meditating away; you might be washing dishes (which is more legitimate in some sense) and meditating away. That may be a genuine way of doing things, but it still feels very suspicious.

Antidotes are any notion that we can do what we want and that as long as we are meditative, everything is going to be fine. The text says to self-liberate even the antidote, the seeming antidote. We may regard going to the movies every minute, every day, every evening as our meditation, or watching television, or grooming our horse, feeding our dog, taking a long walk in the woods. There are endless possibilities like that in the Occidental tradition, or for that matter in the theistic tradition.

The theistic tradition talks about meditation and contemplation as a fantastic thing to do. The popular notion of God is that he created the world: the woods were made by God, the castle ruins were created by God, and the ocean was made by God. So we could swim and meditate or we could lie on the beach made by God and have a fantastic time. Such theistic nature worship has become a problem. We have so many holiday makers, nature worshipers, so many hunters.

In Scotland, at the Samye Ling meditation center, where I was teaching, there was a very friendly neighbor from Birmingham, an industrial town, who always came up there on weekends to have a nice time. Occasionally he would drop into our meditation hall and sit with us, and he would say: "Well, it's nice you people are meditating, but I feel much better if I walk out in the woods with my gun and shoot animals. I feel very meditative walking through the woods and listening to the sharp, subtle sounds of animals jumping forth, and I can shoot at them. I feel I am doing something worthwhile at the same time. I can bring back venison, cook it, and feed my family. I feel good about that."

The whole point of this slogan is that antidotes of any kind, or for that matter occupational therapies of any kind, are not regarded as appropriate things to do. We are not particularly seeking enlightenment or the simple experience of tranquillity—we are trying to get over our deception.

5

Rest in the nature of alaya, the essence.

The idea of this slogan is that in the sitting practice of meditation and with an understanding of ultimate bodhichitta, you actually transcend the seven types of consciousness, and rest in the eighth consciousness, alaya. The first six types of consciousness are the sensory perceptions: [1] visual consciousness, [2] hearing consciousness, [3] smelling consciousness, [4] taste consciousness, [5] feeling or touch consciousness, and [6] mind consciousness, or the basic coordinating factor governing the other five [customarily: eye, ear, nose, tongue, body, and mind consciousness]. The seventh type of consciousness, [7] nuisance mind, is a kind of conglomeration which puts energy into all of that. In Tibetan it is called *nyön-yi: nyön* is short for *nyönmong* [*klesha* in Sanskrit], which literally means "nuisance, "defilements," "neurosis," and *yi* means "mind."

The idea of resting one's mind in the basic alaya is to free oneself from that sevenfold mind and rest in simplicity and in clear and nondiscrimating mind. You begin to feel that sight, smell, sound, and everything else that happens is a production of home ground, or headquarters. You recognize them and then come back to headquarters, where those productions began to manifest. You just rest in the needlessness of those productions.

The idea is that there is a resting place of some kind, which could be called primitive shamatha. There is a starting point, a returning point. You can look at me and as you look at me you might check yourself— but you might check *beyond* yourself and find that some homing device is already taking place. So the idea is to rest in alaya, to be with the homing device, to rest where the orders and information come from.

This whole logic or process is based on taking it for granted that you trust yourself already, to begin with. You have some kind of relaxation with yourself. That is the idea of ultimate bodhichitta. You don't have to run away from yourself all the time in order to get something outside. You can just come home and relax. The idea is to return to home-sweet-home.

You try to give yourself good treatment. You do not follow fixed logic or fixed conceptual ideas of any kind, including discursive thought.

Resting in the nature of alaya means going beyond the six sense consciousnesses, and even beyond the seventh consciousness, the fundamental discursive thought process which brings about the other six. The basic alaya principle goes beyond all that. Even in ordinary situations, if you actually trace back to find out where everything came from, you will find some primitive resting level. You could rest in that primitive basic existence, that existential level.

Starting from the basic alaya principle, we then develop *alaya-vijnana*, or alaya consciousness, which makes distinctions. We begin to create a separation between this and that, who and whom, what and what. That is the notion of consciousness, or we could even call it *self-consciousness*—who is on our side and who is on their side, so to speak. The basic alaya principle does not have any bias. That is why the basic alaya principle is called natural virtue. It is neutral. It is neither male nor female, therefore it is not on either side, and the question of courting is not involved. Alaya *consciousness* is biased. It is either male or female, because the courting concept is involved.

Basic wakefulness, *sugatagarbha*, is beyond alaya, but it goes along with alaya at the same time. It is pre-alaya, but it encompasses the alaya state. Alaya has basic goodness, but sugatagarbha has greater goodness. It is wakefulness in itself. From that point of view, even basic alaya could be said to be consciousness of some kind. Although it is not an official category of consciousness as such, it is a kind of awareness, or maybe even a kind of samsaric mind. But sugatagarbha is beyond that. It is indestructible—the ancestor, or parent, of alaya.

The process of perception, when you first perceive a sense object, has several components. You have the actual mechanisms which perceive things, your physical faculties such as eyes, ears, and so forth. Beyond that are the mental faculties which use those particular instruments to reflect on certain objects. If you go beyond that, there is the intention of doing that, the fascination or inquisitiveness that wants to know how to relate with those objects. And if you go back beyond that altogether, you find there is a basic experience underlying all of that, which is known as the alaya principle.

According to this text on lojong, that experience is known as basic goodness. So this slogan refers to an experience, not simply to the structural, mechanical process of projection. We could describe that process with the analogy of a film projector. We have the screen, the phenomenal world; then we project ourselves onto that phenomenal world; and we have the film, which is the fickleness of mind, constantly changing frames. So we have a moving object projected onto the screen. That moving object is mechanically produced by the machinery of the projector which has lots of teeth to catch the film and mechanical devices to make sure that the projection is continuous—which is precisely the same situation as the sense organs. We look and we listen, therefore when we listen, we look. We connect things together by means of time, although things are shifting completely every moment. And behind the whole thing is the bulb, which projects everything onto the screen. That bulb is the cause of the whole thing. So resting in the nature of alaya is like resting in the nature of that bulb, which is behind the machinery of the film projector. Like the bulb, alaya is brilliant and shining. The bulb does not give in to the fickleness of the rest of the machine. It has no concern with how the screen is coming along or how the image is coming through.

Resting in alaya is the actual practice of ultimate bodhichitta, what happens during sitting practice. You experience ultimate bodhichitta at that level. Ultimate bodhichitta is purely the realization that phenomena cannot be regarded as solid, but at the same time they are self-luminous. In the analogy of the film projector, you have to work with the lamp. You take the lamp out of the projector—there's no monkey business with your projector—and you just screw that lamp onto your regular old-fashioned fixture and look at it. That is the self-liberating alaya.

It may be an embarrassing subject to discuss, but this book is designed for the ordinary practitioner. We are not believing in or cultivating alaya, but we are using it as a stepping stone. It would be dangerous if you cultivated it as an end in itself. In this case it is just another step in the ladder. We are talking very simply about alaya as just a clear mind, a basic clear mind. It is simplicity and clarity and nondiscursive thought—very basic alaya. It may not be completely free from all the consciousnesses, including the eighth consciousness itself, but it is the alaya of basic potentiality.

We have to be very clear on this, generally speaking. We are not trying to grasp the buddha nature immediately, at this point. This instruction on resting in alaya is given to somebody who is at the very beginning level. A lot of us have problems, we have no idea whether we are sitting or not sitting. We have struggles about that. So we are trying to work on our basic premises. It is a slowing-down process. For the first time we learn to slow down.

6

In postmeditation, be a child of illusion.

Being a child of illusion means that in the postmeditation experience there is a sense that everything is based on creating one's basic perceptions out of one's preconceptions. If you can cut through that and inject some basic understanding or awareness, you begin to see that the games going on are not even big games but simply illusory ones. To realize that requires a lot of mindfulness and awareness working together. Here we are talking about meditation in action, actually, or postmeditation discipline.

Illusion does not mean haziness, confusion, or mirage. Being a child of illusion means that you continue what you have experienced in your sitting practice [resting in the nature of alaya] into postmeditation experience. Continuing with the analogy of the projector, during postmeditation you take the bulb out. You might not have the screen or the film at this point, but you transfer the bulb into your flashlight and carry it with you all the time.

You realize that after you finish sitting practice, you do not have to solidify phenomena. Instead, you can continue your practice and develop some kind of ongoing awareness. If things become heavy and solid, you flash mindfulness and awareness into them. In that way you begin to see that everything is pliable and workable. Your attitude is that the phenomenal world is not evil, that "they" are not going to attack you or destroy you or kill you. Everything is workable and soothing.

It is like swimming: you swim along in your phenomenal world. You can't just float, you have to swim; you have to use your limbs. That process of using your limbs is the basic stroke of mindfulness and awareness. It is the "flash" quality of it—you flash on to things. So you are swimming constantly in postmeditarion. And during meditation, you just sit and rest in the nature of your alaya, very simply. That is how we could develop ultimate bodhichitta. It is very basic and ordinary. You can actually do it. That's the whole idea.

It is not abstract, you simply look at phenomena and see their padded-wall quality, if you like. That's the illusion: padded walls everywhere. You think you are just about to strike against something very sharp, while having a cup of tea, or whatever, and you find that things bounce back on you. There is not so much sharp contrast—everything is part of your mindfulness and awareness. Everything bounces back, like the ball in one of those little television Ping-Pong games. When it returns, you might throw it out again by not being a child of illusion, but it comes back again with a beep, so you become a child of illusion. It is "first thought, best thought." When you look at things, you find that they are soft and that they bounce back on you all the time. It's not particularly intellectual.

This slogan is about learning how to nurture ultimate bodhichitta in terms of mindfulness and awareness. We have to learn how we can actually experience that things in the postmeditation situation are still workable, that there is room, lots of space. The basic idea of being a child of illusion is that we don't feel claustrophobic. After your sitting practice, you might think, "Oh boy, now I have to do the postmeditation practices." But you don't have to feel that you are closed in. Instead you can feel that you are a child of illusion, that you are dancing around and clicking with those little beeps, all the time. It is fresh and simple and very effective. The point is to treat yourself better. If you want to take a vacation from your practice, you can do so and still remain a child of illusion. Things just keep on beeping at you all the time. It's very lucid. It's almost whimsical.

Being a child of illusion is very simple. It is being willing to realize the simplicity of phenomenal play and to use that simplicity as a part of awareness and mindfulness practice. It's a very strong phrase, "child of illusion." Think about it. Try to be one. You have plenty of opportunities.

RELATIVE BODHICHITTA SLOGANS

7

Sending and taking should be practiced alternately. These two should ride the breath.

Sending and taking is a very important practice of the bodhisattva path. It is called *tonglen* in Tibetan: *tong* means "sending out" or "letting go," and *len* means "receiving," or "accepting." *Tonglen* is a very important term; you should remember it. It is the main practice in the development of relative bodhichitta.

The slogan says: "These two should ride the breath." We have been using the breath as a technique all along because it is constant and because it is something very natural to us. Therefore, we also use it here, in exactly the same way as we have been doing in shamatha discipline.

The practice of tonglen is quite straightforward; it is an actual sitting meditation practice. You give away your happiness, your pleasure, anything that feels good. All of that goes out with the outbreath. As you breathe in, you breathe in any resentments and problems, anything that feels bad. The whole point is to remove territoriality altogether.

The practice of tonglen is very simple. We do not first have to sort out our doctrinal definitions of goodness and evil. We simply breathe out any old good and breathe in any old bad. At first we may seem to be relating primarily to our *ideas* of good and bad. But as we go on, it becomes more real. On the one hand, you can't expect a friendly letter from your grandmother with whom you have been engaged in warfare for the past five years. She probably will not write you a kind letter after three days of tonglen. On the other hand, sending and taking will definitely have a good effect, quite naturally. I think it is a question of your general decorum and attitude.

Sometimes we feel terrible that we are breathing in poison which might kill us and at the same time breathing out whatever little goodness we have. It seems to be completely impractical. But once we begin to break through, we realize that we have even more goodness and we also have more things to breathe in. So the whole process becomes somewhat balanced. That always happens, but it takes long training. Sending and taking are interdependent. The more negativity we take in with a sense of openness and compassion the more goodness there is to breathe out on the other side. So there is nothing to lose. It is all one process.

In tonglen we are aspiring to take on the suffering of other sentient beings. We mean that literally: we are actually willing to take that on. As such, it can have real effects, both on the practitioner himself and on others. There is a story about a great Kadampa teacher who was practicing tonglen and who actually did take another's pain on himself: when somebody stoned a dog outside his house, the teacher himself was bruised. And the same kind of thing could happen to us. But tonglen should not be used as any kind of antidote. You do not do it and then wait for the effect—you just do it and drop it. It doesn't matter whether it works or not: if it works, you breathe that out; if it does not work, you breathe that in. So you do not possess anything. That is the point.

Usually you would like to hold on to your goodness. You would like to make a fence around yourself and put everything bad outside it: foreigners, your neighbors, or what have you. You don't want them to come in. You don't even want your neighbors to walk their dogs on your property because they might make a mess on your lawn. So in ordinary samsaric life, you don't send and receive at all. You try as much as possible to guard those pleasant little situations you have created for yourself. You try to put them in a vacuum, like fruit in a tin, completely purified and clean. You try to hold on to as much as you can, and anything outside of your territory is regarded as altogether problematic. You don't want to catch the local influenza or the local diarrhea attack that is going around. You are constantly trying to ward off as much as you can. You may not have enough money to build a castle or a wall around you, but your front door is very reliable. You are always putting double locks on it. Even when you check into a hotel, the management always tells you to double-lock your door and not to let anybody come in unless you check them out first. You can read that in the Innkeepers Act posted on the back of hotel doors. That will probably tell you the whole thing. Aren't we crazy?

Basically speaking, the mahayana path is trying to show us that we don't have to secure ourselves. We can afford to extend out a little bit— quite a bit. The basic idea of practicing sending and taking is almost a rehearsal, a discipline of passionlessness, a way of overcoming territory. Overcoming territory consists of going out with the out-breath, giving away and sending out, and bringing in with your in-breath as much as you can of other people's pain and misery. You would like to become the object of that pain and misery. You want to experience it fully and thoroughly.

You practice putting others first by means of a very literal discipline, called tonglen. How are you going to do that in the ordinary sense? Should you just run up to somebody in the street and say, "Hey, take my candy and give me the Kleenex in your pocket?" Of course, you could do that if you like, and if you were versatile enough, you could probably do it without offending anybody. But that is experimenting with others on a very crude level. What we are doing is different. We have a way of practicing putting others first—by placing letting go and receiving on the medium of the breath. The first stage of tonglen consists of the practice of sending and taking mentally, psychologically, slowly and slowly. Then at the end one might actually *do* such a thing. It has been said in the scriptures that one can even practice tonglen by taking a piece of fruit in one hand and giving it to the other hand.

There are obviously a lot of obstacles to practicing tonglen, particularly since we are involved in modern industrial society. But you can do it step by step, which actually makes you grow up and become the ultimate adult. The main point is to develop the psychological attitude of exchanging oneself for others: instead of being John Doe, you could become Joe Schmidt. You might have a lot of pride and reservations, but nonetheless you can begin to do that. Obviously, to begin with, tonglen is more of a psychological state than anything else. If everybody began to give things away to each other, there would be tremendous conflict. But if you develop the attitude of being willing to part with your precious things, to give away your precious things to others, that can help begin to create a good reality.

How do we actually practice tonglen? First we think about our parents, or our friends, or anybody who has sacrificed his or her life for our benefit. In many cases, we have never even said thank you to them. It is very important to think about that, not in order to develop guilt but just to realize how mean we have been. We always said, "I want," and they did so much for us, without any complaint.

I'm sure you have a lot of stories about how badly you treated your parents and friends, who helped you so much. They dedicated their entire being for your sake, and you never even bothered to say thank you or write them a letter. You should think of the people who cared for you so much that they didn't even look for confirmation. There are many people like that. Sometimes somebody comes along out of the blue and tries to help you completely. Such people do everything for you—they serve you, they sacrifice themselves, and then they go away without even leaving an address or a number to call. All along there have been people who have done things for you. You should think of those situations and work them into your tonglen practice. As your breath goes out, you give them the best of what is yours, in order to repay their kindness. In order to promote goodness in the world, you give out everything good, the best that you have, and you breathe in other people's problems, their misery, their torment. You take in their pain on their behalf.

That is the basic idea of relative bodhichitta practice. It is a very action-oriented practice. We give as much as we can give, we expand as much as we can expand. We have a lot to expand because we have basic goodness, which is an inexhaustible treasure. Therefore we have nothing at all to lose and we can receive more, also. We can be shock absorbers of other people's pain all the time. It is a very moving practice — not that I'm saying we are all in a train, particularly. The more we give our best, the more we are able to receive other people's worst. Isn't that great?

Tonglen seems to be one of the best measures we could take to solve our problems of ecology and pollution. Since everything is included, tonglen is the fundamental way to solve the pollution problem—it is the only way. Quite possibly it will have the physical effect of cleaning up pollution in big cities, maybe even in the entire world. That possibility is quite powerful.

Sending and taking is not regarded as proof of our personal bravery. It is not that we are the best people because we do tonglen. Sending and taking is regarded as a natural course of exchange; it just takes place. We might have difficulty taking in pollution, taking in what is bad, but we should take it in wholeheartedly—completely in. We should begin to feel that our lungs are altogether filled with bad air, that we have actually cleaned out the world out there and taken it into ourselves. Then some switch takes place, and as we breathe out, we find that we still have an enormous treasure of good breath which goes out all the time.

We start by thinking of our own mother or parents, of somebody we really love so much, care for so much, like our mother, who nursed us, took care of us, paid attention to us, and brought us up to this level of grown-upness. Such affection and kindness was radiated to us by that person that we think of her first. The analogy of our mother is not necessarily the only way. The idea is that of a motherly person who was kind and gentle and patient to us. We must have somebody who is gentle, somebody who has been kind to us in our life and who shared his or her goodness with us. If we do not have that, then we are somewhat in trouble, we begin to hate the world—but there is also a measure for that, which is to breathe in our hatred and resentment of the world. If we do not have good parents, a good mother, or a good person who reflected such a kind attitude toward us to think about, then we can think of ourselves.

When you begin to do tonglen practice, you begin to think of the goodness that you can give out, what you can give to others. You have lots of good things to give, to breathe out to others. You have lots of goodness, lots of sanity, lots of healthiness. All of that comes straight from the basic awakened and enlightened attitude, which is alive and strong and powerful. So what you give out is no longer just imagination, or something that you have to crank up; you actually have something good to give out to somebody. In turn, you can breathe in something that is painful and negative. The suffering that other people are experiencing can be brought in because, in contrast to that, you have basic healthiness and wakefulness, which can certainly absorb anything that comes to it. You can absorb more suffering because you have a lot more to give.

The idea of warmth is a basic principle of tonglen practice. What we are doing is also called maitri practice, or in Sanskrit, *maitri bhavana*. *Maitri* means "friendliness," "warmth," or "sympathy," and *bhavana* means "meditation" or "practice." In tonglen, or maitri bhavana, we breathe out anything gentle and kind, feeling good about anything at all—even feeling good about eating a chocolate cake or drinking cool water or warming ourselves by the fire. Whatever goodness exists in us, whatever we feel good about, we breathe out to others. We must feel good sometimes—whether it lasts a minute or a second or whatever. And then we breathe in the opposite situation, whatever is bad and terrible, gross and obnoxious. We try to breathe that into ourselves.

I would like to say quite bluntly that it is very important for you to take tonglen practice quite seriously. I doubt that you will freak out. The main point is actually to do it properly and thoroughly. Beyond that, it is important to take delight that you are in a position to do something which most other humans never do at all. The problem with most people is that they are always trying to give out the bad and take in the good. That has been the problem of society in general and the world altogether. But now we are on the mahayana path and the logic is reversed. That is fantastic, extraordinary! We are actually getting the inner "scoop," so to speak, on Buddha's mind, directly and at its best. Please think of that. This practice will be extremely helpful to you, so please take it seriously.

Tonglen practice is not purely mind training. What you are doing might be real! When you practice, you have to be very literal: when you breathe out, you really breathe out good; when you breathe in, you really breathe in bad. We can't be faking.

Start with what is immediate. Just this. *This.* You should feel that the whole thing is loose. Nothing is really attached to you or anchored to you; everything is detachable. When you let go, it is all gone. When things come back to you, they too are unanchored, from an outsider's point of view. They come to you, and you go out to them. It is a very exciting experience, actually. You feel a tremendous sense of space.

When you let go it is like cutting a kite from its cord. But even without its cord, the kite still comes back, like a parachute landing on you. You feel a sense of fluidity and things begin to circulate so wonderfully. Nothing is being dealt with in any form of innuendo, or in undercurrents. There is no sense of someone working the politics behind the scenes. Everything is completely free-flowing. It is so wonderful—and you can do it. That is precisely what we mean when we talk about genuineness. You can be so absolutely blatantly good at giving, and so good at taking. It is interesting.

In tonglen practice, we replace the mindfulness of the breath that doesn't have any contents with the mindfulness of the breath that does. The contents are the emotional, discursive thoughts which are being given the reference point of people's pain and pleasure. So you are supposed to actually be working hard for the sake of other people. You are supposed to be helping people. If somebody is bleeding in front of you, you can't just stand there holding the bandages—you are supposed to run over and put bandages on him, for goodness' sake! You just do it. And then you come back and sit down and watch to see who else might need bandages. It is as simple as that. It is the first-aid approach.

People need help. So we have to wake up a little bit more. We have to be careful that we don't just regard this as another daydream or concept. We have to make it very literal and very ordinary. Just breathe out and in. It is very literal, very straightforward. Discursiveness doesn't take over—unless you are possessed by a demon or the ghost of Julius Caesar or something like that. Just make it very direct, very literal and regimented. Your breathing goes out for *that*, your breathing comes in for *this—that, this, that, this*. You breathe out good and breathe in bad. It is very simple and very literal.

You don't practice tonglen and then wait for the effect. You just do it and then drop it. You don't look for results. Whether it works or not, you just do it and drop it, do it and drop it. If it doesn't work, you take in, and if it works, you give out. So you do not possess anything. That is the whole idea. When anything comes out well, you give it away; if anything does not work out, you take it in.

Tonglen practice is not a very subtle thing. It is not philosophical, it is not even psychological. It is a very, very simple-minded approach. The practice is very primitive, in fact, the most primitive of all Buddhist practices. When you think of Buddhism and all the sophisticated wisdom, philosophies, and techniques that have been developed, it is amazing that they came up with this practice, that we do such a simple and primitive thing. But we do it and it works. It seems to have been fine for several centuries, and those centuries have produced a lot of bodhisattvas, including Buddha himself.

Just relate with the technique; the discursiveness of it doesn't matter. When you go out, you are out; when you come in, you are in. When you are hot, you are hot; when you are cool, you are cool. Just cut into that situation and be very precise. Make it very literal and very simple. We don't want to make this into a revolutionary sort of imaginary, mind-oriented social work approach or psychological approach. Let's do it properly.

We have to be honest to begin with. That is a very important point. And we have to be very literal with the technique. It has already been worked on by generations of people in the past, and it has proven to be true. So we can afford to be literal. We don't have to research it any further. Instead we could be quite faithful to the practice as it is and just do it for a while. Then we might discover the impact of that and we could go on from there. Suddenly, we might find that we could attain enlightenment.

Sending and taking is just like field training, actually. It is like soldiers learning how to puncture a bag full of sand: regarding that as the enemy, they yell, "Hooooh!" [Vidyadhara makes slashing motion with fan], as they pierce that bag of sand with their bayonets. A lot of soldiers might have a hard time being involved with nature because they come from cities where people have no idea how to work with snow or the heat of summer; they don't know how to ford rivers or how to dry their clothes or how to work with dirt and cleanliness, so soldiers have to be trained in the field. In a similar way, warriors who follow the bodhisattva path go through the same kind of field training.

If we begin to get hurt by being genuine, that is good. That is the level at which we are capable of exchanging ourselves for others. We begin to feel that because we are doing such genuine, honest work we would like to invite others. It is not so much that we only want to give out our pleasure to others and bring in their pain. There is more to it than that. We want to give our genuineness out to others and we want to invite their hypocrisy into us. That is much more than just exchanging pain for pleasure. It is the greatest way of exchanging ourselves for others, and it is needed in the world very, very badly. Exchanging pain for pleasure is very simple and easy to do. For instance, someone across the street would like to take a hot bath, but when he jumps into the water, it is cold. So you might say, "Come over here and jump into my hot bath with me. You jump into my hot bath and I'll jump into your cold bath." That is fine, there is no problem with that—but jumping into each other's hypocrisy is more interesting. That is what we are trying to do.

Our genuineness has to be shared with someone. It has to be given up. Genuineness shouldn't be regarded as our one and only family jewel that we want to hang on to. We have to give our genuineness away to someone. We don't particularly lose it that way; instead, we bring other people's deception into us, and we work on our own genuineness along with that. So exchanging ourselves for others is something more than we might have thought. It is more than just jumping from a hot bath to a cold bath.

Beyond that, you begin to develop a sense of joy. You are actually doing something very useful and workable and fundamentally wonderful. You are not only teaching yourself how to be unselfish, in the conventional sense, but you are also teaching the world how to overcome hypocrisy, which is becoming thicker and thicker lately as the world gets more and more sophisticated, so to speak—more and more into the dark ages, in other words.

Sending and taking is an extension of shamatha discipline. In shamatha discipline, we do not dwell on anything, but we are processed by working with movement. We don't just try to hold our mind completely steady, completely settled, but we try to use the fickleness of our mental process by following our breath and by looking at our subconscious thoughts. We develop bodhichitta in exactly the same way that we practice shamatha, only our practice in this case is much more highlighted because, instead of working with subconscious mind or discur-sive thoughts alone, we are looking much further, to the *content* of our thoughts, which is either anger or lust or stupidity. So we are going slightly beyond shamatha technique, to include the contents of these thoughts.

The whole thing is that for a long time we have wanted to inflict pain on others and cultivate pleasure for ourselves. That has been the problem all along. In this case, we are reversing the logic altogether to see what happens. Instead of inflicting pain on others, we take on the pain ourselves; instead of sucking out others' pleasure, we give our pleasure to them. We have been doing the usual samsaric thing all the time, so we are just trying to reverse samsaric logic a little bit to see what happens. And what usually happens is that you become a gentle person. You don't become demonic, you become workable. You see, you have been so unreasonable all along that now, in order to make yourself a reasonable person, you have to overdo the whole thing slightly. By doing so, you begin to realize how to be a decent person. That is called relative bodhichitta. At this point, it is important to have that particular kind of experience, it is important to understand your unreasonability.

Tonglen is also very important in terms of vajrayana practice. Therefore, vajrayana practitioners should also pay heed to this practice. They should do it very carefully. Without tonglen, you cannot practice the vajrayana disciplines of *utpattikrama* [developing stage] and *sampannakrama* [completion stage] at all. You become a deity without a heart, just a papier-mâché deity.[2] There is a story about two vajrayana masters who were exchanging notes on their students. One said, "My students can perform miracles, but somehow after that they seem to lose heart. They become ordinary people." The other one said, "Strangely enough, my vajrayana students cannot perform miracles, but they always remain healthy." The two teachers discussed that question on and on. Then somebody said, "Well, how about having all of them practice tonglen?" Both teachers laughed and said, "Ha! That must be it." From that point of view, it is very important for us to have a basic core of reality taking place, so that when we do vajrayana practice, we don't just dress up as deities, with masks and costumes.

Even in hinayana practice, we could just wear our monks' robes and shave our heads, and all the rest of it. Without tonglen practice, both hinayana and vajrayana become like the lion's corpse. [Because the lion is the king of beasts, when he dies, it is said that his corpse is not attacked by other animals, but is left to be eaten by maggots from within.] As the Buddha said, his teaching will not be destroyed by outsiders but by insiders who do not practice the true dharma. At that point the Buddha was definitely referring to the bodhisattva path. It is the mahayana tradition and discipline that hold the hinayana and vajrayana together. Please think of that.

8

Three objects, three poisons, and three seeds of virtue.

This slogan is connected with the postmeditation experience which comes after the main practice. Relating to passion, aggression, and ignorance in the main practice of tonglen is very intense, but the postmeditation practice is somewhat lighter.

The three objects are friends, enemies, and neutrals. The three poisons are passion, aggression, and ignorance or delusion. And the three seeds of virtue are the absence of passion, aggression, and ignorance.

The practice of this slogan is to take the passion, aggression, and delusion of others upon ourselves so that they may be free and undefiled. Passion is wanting to magnetize or possess; aggression is wanting to reject, attack, cast out; and ignorance or indifference is that you couldn't be bothered, you are not interested, a kind of anti-*prajna* energy. We take upon ourselves the aggression of our enemies, the passion of our friends, and the indifference of the neutrals.

When we reflect on our enemy, that inspires aggression. Whatever aggression our enemy has provided for us—let that aggression be ours and let the enemy thereby be free from any kind of aggression. Whatever passion has been created by our friends, let us take that neurosis into ourselves and let our friends be freed from passion. And the indifference of those who are in the middle or unconcerned, those who are ignorant, deluded, or noncaring, let us bring that neurosis into ourselves and let those people be free from ignorance.

Whenever any of the three poisons happens in your life, you should do the sending and taking practice. You just look at your passion, your aggression, and your delusion—you do not regard them as a problem or as a promise. Instead, when you are in a state of aggression, you say: "May this aggression be a working base for me. May I learn to hold my aggression to myself, and may all sentient beings thereby attain freedom from aggression." Or: "May this passion be mine. Because it belongs to me by virtue of my holding on to it, therefore may others be free of such passion." For indifference, you do the same thing.

The purpose of doing that is that when you begin to hold the three poisons as yours, when you possess them fully and completely, when you take charge of them fully, you will find, interestingly enough, that the logic is reversed. If you have no object of aggression, you cannot hold your own aggression purely by yourself. If you have no object of passion, you cannot hold your passion yourself. And in the same way, you cannot hold on to your ignorance either.

By holding your poison, you let go of the object, or the intent, of your poison. You see, what usually happens is that you have objects of the three poisons. When you have an object of aggression, for example, you feel angry toward it—right? But if your anger is not directed *toward* something, the object of aggression falls apart. It is impossible to have an object of anger, because the anger belongs to you rather than to its object. You give your compassion to the object so that it doesn't provoke your anger—then what are you angry with? You find yourself just hanging out there, with no one to project onto. Therefore, you can cut the root of the three poisons by dealing with others rather than by dealing with yourself. So an interesting twist takes place.

9

In all activities, train with slogans.

This slogan, which is connected with postmeditation practice, is very interesting and important. We have been using this technique all the time, throughout our practice. Particularly in dharmic environments, wherever we have a wall we post the slogans in order to remind ourselves of them. The point is to catch the first thought. It is not all that simple-minded. The idea is that in catching the first thought, that first thought should have some words.

In this case, whenever you feel that quality of me-ness, whenever you feel "I"—and maybe "am" as well—then you should think of these two sayings: [1] May I receive all evils; may my virtues go to others. [2] Profit and victory to others; loss and defeat to myself.[3] It doesn't have to be verbalized, but it is a thought process: whenever you have a sense of yuckiness, you make it your property; whenever you have a sense of vision or upliftedness, you give it to others. So there is that sort of black and white contrast: black and white, nausea and relaxation, feeling ugly and feeling pretty. [Vidyadhara flips his hand back and forth.] That flip takes place very simply. When there is "I," you take it—when there is "am," you give it. It takes quite a lot of effort because it is a big job. That is why it is called the mahayana [big vehicle], it is a big deal. You can not fall asleep at the wheel when you are driving on this big highway. It takes quite a lot of effort! It is no joke. You can't go wrong with such heavy-handedness. It is the best kind of heavy-handedness that has ever occurred. It's no joke.

10

Begin the sequence of sending and taking with yourself.

The way we often express this idea is, "First thought, best thought." Usually we have the feeling that *this* happens first, before other, or *that*. So whenever anything happens, the first thing to do is to take on the pain yourself. Afterward, you give away anything which is left beyond that, anything pleasurable. We are not necessarily talking about plea- surable in the sense of feeling extraordinarily good—but anything other than pain is given away. So you do not hold on to any possible way of entertaining yourself or giving yourself good treatments

This slogan is connected with giving up passion, as it is passion which makes you demand pleasure for yourself. Therefore, this slogan is also connected very vividly and closely with the paramita of disci- pline. We are not talking about masochism, or about killing or de- stroying yourself. But you begin to realize that anything connected with the demands of wanting and not wanting is constantly involved with the desire to possess and not to give out. So the whole approach here is to open your territory completely, to let go of everything. If you sud- denly discover that a hundred hippies want to camp in your living room, let them do so! But then those hippies also have to practice.

The basic idea of this practice is actually very joyful. It is wonder- ful that human beings can do such a fantastic exchange and that they are willing to invite such undesirable situations into their world. It is wonderful that they are willing to let go of even their smallest corners of secrecy and privacy, so that their holding on to anything is gone com- pletely. That is very brave. We could certainly say that this is the world of the warrior, from the bodhisattva's point of view.

POINT THREE

Transformation of Bad Circumstances into the Path of Enlightenment

POINT THREE AND THE PARAMITA OF PATIENCE

Now that we have studied the ultimate and relative bodhichitta practices and the postmeditation experiences connected with them, the third group of slogans is connected with how to carry out all those practices as path. In Tibetan this group of slogans is known as *lamkhyer*: *lam* meaning "path" and *khyer* meaning "carrying." In other words, whatever happens in your life should be included as part of your journey. That is the basic idea.

This group of slogans is connected with paramita of patience. The definition of patience is forbearance. Whatever happens, you don't react to it. The obstacle to patience is aggression. Patience does not mean biding your time and trying to slow down. Impatience arises when you become too sensitive and you don't have any way to deal with your environment, your atmosphere. You feel very touchy, very sensitive. So the paramita of patience is often described as a suit of armor. Patience has a sense of dignity and forbearance. You are not so easily disturbed by the world's aggression.

II

When the world is filled with evil,
Transform all mishaps into the path of bodhi.

Continuing with the idea of carrying everything to the path, the basic slogan of this section is:

> When the world is filled with evil,
> Transform all mishaps into the path of bodhi.

That is to say, whatever occurs in your life—environmental problems, political problems, or psychological problems—should be transformed into a part of your wakefulness, or bodhi. Such wakefulness is a result of the practice of shamatha-vipashyana discipline as well as your basic understanding of soft spot, or bodhichitta.

In other words, you do not blame the environment or the world political situation. Certain people are inspired to write poetry and act in such a way that they sacrifice their lives for a social cause. We could quite safely say that the Vietnam War produced a lot of poets and philosophers, but their work is not in keeping with this mahayana principle. They were purely reacting against the world being filled with evil; they were not able to transform mishaps into the path of bodhi. Such poets may even regard evil as material for their writing. If the Vietnam War had never happened, we would have fewer of such poets and philosophers. According to this slogan, when the world is filled with evil, or even when the world is not filled with evil, any mishaps that might occur should all be transformed into the path of bodhi, or wakefulness. That understanding comes from your sitting practice and your general awareness.

This slogan says practically everything about how we can practice generosity as well. In our ordinary life, our immediate surroundings or our once-removed surroundings are not necessarily hospitable. There are always problems and difficulties. There are difficulties even for those who proclaim that their lives are very successful, those who have become the president of their country, or the richest millionaires, or the most famous poets or movie stars or surfers or bullfighters. Even if our lives go right, according to our expectations, there are still difficulties. Obstacles always arise. That is something everybody experiences. And when obstacles happen, any mishaps connected with those obstacles—poverty mentality, fixating on loss and gain, or any kind of competitiveness—should be transformed into the path of bodhi.

That is a very powerful and direct message. It is connected with not feeling poverty stricken all the time. You might feel inadequate because you have a sick father and a crazy mother and you have to take care of them, or because you have a distorted life and money problems. For that matter, even if you have a successful life and everything is going all right, you might feel inadequate because you have to work constantly to maintain your business. A lot of those situations could be regarded as expressions of your own timidity and cowardice. They could all be regarded as expressions of your poverty mentality.

Having already experienced the possibilities of absolute and relative bodhichitta, and practiced sending and taking, you should also begin to build up confidence and joy in your own richness. That richness is the essence of generosity. It is the sense of resourcefulness, that you can deal with whatever is available around you and not feel poverty stricken. Even if you are abandoned in the middle of a desert and you want a pillow, you can find a piece of rock with moss on it that is quite comfortable to put your head on. Then you can lie down and have a good sleep. Having such a sense of resourcefulness and richness seems to be the main point. Practicing that resourcefulness and richness, or generosity, is the way to become mahayanists, or even vajrayanists.

We have found that a lot of people complain that they are involved in intense domestic situations: they relate with everything in their lives purely on the level of pennies, tiny stitches, drops of water, grains of rice. But we do not have to do that—we can expand our vision by means of generosity. We can give something to others. We don't always have to receive something first in order to give something away. Having connected with the notion of generosity, we begin to realize a sense of wealth automatically. The nature of generosity is to be free from desire, free from attachment, able to let go of anything.

This slogan is the basic statement of the third point of lojong practices Within this category, we have three further practices. The next two slogans are connected with the practice of relative bodhichitta, how to carry what occurs in your life onto the path of relative bodhichitta. Slogan 14 ["Seeing confusion as the four kayas / Is unsurpassable shunyata protection"] is connected with absolute bodhichitta practice, how you carry that out as your path. And the final slogan in this section [slogan 15] is connected with the particular actions that enable you to carry whatever occurs in your practice onto the path.

12

Drive all blames into one.

This slogan is about dealing with conventional reality, or *kündzop*. No matter what appears in our ordinary experience, whatever trips we might be involved in, whatever interesting and powerful situations—we do not have any expectations in return for our kindness. When we are kind to somebody, there are no expectations that there will be any reward for that. Drive all blames into one means that all the problems and the complications that exist around our practice, realization, and understanding are not somebody else's fault. All the blame always starts with ourselves.

A lot of people seem to get through this world and actually make quite a comfortable life by being compassionate and open—even seemingly compassionate and open. They seem to get along in this world. Yet although we share the same kind of world, we ourselves get hit constantly. We get blamed and we get into trouble—emotional problems, financial problems, domestic, relationship, and sociological problems are happening all the time. What is playing tricks on us? A popular phrase says, "Don't lay your trip on me." Interestingly, trips *are* laid on us, but not *by* anybody. We decide to take on those trips ourselves, and then we become resentful and angry.

We might have entirely the same lifestyle as somebody else. For instance, we could be sharing a room with a college mate, eating the same problematic food, sharing the same shitty house, having the same schedule and the same teachers. Our roommate manages to handle everything okay and find his or her freedom. We, on the other hand, are stuck with that memory and filled with resentment all the time. We would like to be revolutionary, to blow up the world. But who did that to us? We could say that the schoolteacher did it, that everybody hates us and they did it. But *why* do they hate us? That is a very interesting point.

The blame for every mishap that happens to us is always directed naturally to us; it is our particular doing. This is not just purely mahayana wishy-washy thinking. You might say that what we are discussing tonight is purely mahayana—once we get into tantra, we might get revenge on those people. But that doesn't work. I would request you not to try that. Everything is based on our own uptightness. We could blame the organization; we could blame the government; we could blame the police force; we could blame the weather; we could blame the food; we could blame the highways; we could blame our own motorcars, our own clothes; we could blame an infinite variety of things. But it is we who are not letting go, not developing enough warmth and sympathy—which makes us problematic. So we cannot blame anybody.

Of course, we could build up all kinds of philosophies and think we are representing the voice of the rest of the world, saying that this is the world's opinion, that is what happens in the a world. "Don't you see that you should not make me suffer this? The world is this way, the true world is that way." But we are *not* speaking on behalf of the world, we are simply speaking on behalf of ourselves.

This slogan applies whenever we complain about anything, even that our coffee is cold or the bathroom is dirty. It goes very far. Everything is due to our own uptightness, so to speak, which is known as ego holding, ego fixation. Since we are so uptight about ourselves, that makes us very vulnerable at the same time. We consequently provide the ideal target. We get hit, but nobody means to hit us—we are actually inviting the bullets. So there we are, in the good old world. Driving all blames into one is a very good idea.

The intention of driving all blames into one is that otherwise you will not enter the bodhisattva path. Therefore, you do not want to lay any emotional, aggressive blame on anybody at all. So driving all blames into one begins with that attitude. On that basis, you drive all blames into one again at the level of vipashyana. This involves actually experiencing the real, visible, logical consequences of doing otherwise.

For instance, you could drive all blames into Joe Schmidt, but instead you drive all blames into yourself. In this case, you actually begin to see the possibility that aggression and neurosis are expanded if you drive your neurosis into somebody else. So instead, you drive your blames onto yourself. That is the basic point.

All of this seems to come under the general categories of compassion for others and having a loving attitude to oneself, known in Sanskrit as karuna and maitri. In other words, the experience of karuna and maitri is to drive all blames into one. So this slogan is connected with the basic discipline of the bodhisattva path, which is to refrain from any kind of ill-doing. The traditional listing of the forty-six ways in which a bodhisattva fails [see Appendix] could be used in connection with driving all blames into one. They are connected very basically.

This slogan is the essence of the bodhisattva path. Even though somebody else has made a terrible boo-boo and blamed it on you, you should take the blame yourself. In terms of power, it is a much simpler and more direct way of controlling the situation. In addition, it is most direct way of simplifying complicated neuroses into one point. Also, if you look for volunteers around you to take the blame, there will be no volunteers other than yourself. By taking that particular blame on yourself, you reduce the neurosis that's happening around you. You also reduce any paranoia existing in other people, so that those people might have clearer vision.

You can actually say, "I take the blame. It's my fault that such and such a thing happened and that such and such things took place as a result." It is very simple and ordinary. You can actually communicate with somebody who is not in a defensive mood, since you already took all the blame. It is much better and easier to talk to somebody when you have accepted the blame already. Then you can clarify the situation, and quite possibly the person you are talking to, who might be the cause of the particular problem, would realize that he has done something terrible himself. He might recognize his own wrongdoing. But it helps that the blame, which is just a paper tiger at that point, has already been taken on by you. That helps.

This kind of approach becomes very powerfully important. I've actually done it thousands of times. I've taken a lot of blame personally. A person may actually do a terrible thing based on his or her understanding of my recommendation. But that's okay, I can take it on wholeheartedly as my problem. In that way there is some chance of working with such a person, and the person begins to go along and fulfill his actions properly, and everything is fine.

That's a tip for bureaucrats. If individuals can take the blame themselves and let their friends off to continue their work or duty, that will make the whole organization work better and allow it to be much more functional. When you say, "You're full of shit! I didn't do such a thing. It wasn't me, it's you who did it. There's no blame on me," the whole thing gets very complicated. You begin to find this little plop of a dirty thing bouncing around in the bureaucracy, something like a football bouncing back and forth. And if you fight over it too much, you have tremendous difficulty dissolving or resolving that particular block, plop, slug. So the earlier you take the blame, the better. And although it is not really, fundamentally your fault at all, you should take it as if it's yours.

This seems to be the interesting point where the two aspects of the bodhisattva vow, *mönpa* and *jukpa* [desiring to enter and actually entering into bodhisattva discipline] come together. It is how you work with your fellow sentient beings. If you do not allow a little bit of blame and injustice to come to you, nothing is going to work. And if you do not really absorb all the blame, but say it is not yours since you are too good and are doing so well, then nothing is going to work. This is so because everybody is looking for someone to blame, and they would like to blame *you*—not because you have done anything, but because they probably think you have a soft spot in your heart. They think that if they put their jam or honey or glue on you, then you actually might buy it and say, "Okay, the blame is mine."

Once you begin to do that, it is the highest and most powerful logic, the most powerful incantation you can make. You can actually make the whole thing functional. You can absorb the poison—then the rest of the situation becomes medicine. If nobody is willing to absorb the blame, it becomes a big interrelational football. It is not even tight like a good football, but filled with a lot of glue and gooey all over the outside as well. Everybody tries to pass it on to each other and nothing happens. Finally that football begins to grow bigger and bigger and bigger and bigger. Then it causes revolutions and all the rest.

As far as international politics are concerned, somebody is always trying to put the blame on somebody else, to pass that huge, overbuilt, gooey, dirty, smelly, gigantic football with all sorts of worms coming out of it. People say, "It's not mine, it's yours." The communists say it belongs to the capitalists and the capitalists say it belongs to the communists. Throwing it back and forth doesn't help anyone at all. So even from the point of view of political theory—if there is such a thing as politics in the mahayana or in Buddhism—it is important for individuals to absorb unjustified blame and to work with that. It is very important and necessary.

Such an approach is neither very theistic and Occidental nor is it Oriental. But it is possible to do, which is one of the interesting points about nontheism. If you are in a theistic discipline, you don't actually take the blame. Supposedly this guy up in the sky with the beard and big nose says that when you're right, you're right, so fight for your right; and when you're wrong, you just repent. You should do your duty and all that. So much for that old hat. But for a lot of people, this may be a new hat, actually. You could freak out and say, "Do you mean to say that I should take the blame for somebody else? I should get myself killed for that?" You don't have to go so far as to do that—but you actually can accommodate that much blame. You can do that.

Usually, with any problems at all that might occur in your life— political, environmental, psychological, or, for that matter, domestic or spiritual—you always decide to blame it on somebody else. You may not have a particular individual to blame, but you still come up with the basic logic that something is wrong. You might go to the authorities or your political leaders or your friends and demand that the environment be changed. That is your usual way of complaining to people. You might organize a group of people who, like yourself, blame the environment, and you might collect signatures for a petition and give it to some leader who might be able to change the environment. Or, for that matter, your complaint might be purely individual: if your husband or wife is in love with somebody else, you might ask him or her to give up his or her lover. But as far as you yourself are concerned, you feel so pure and good, you never touch yourself at all. You want to maintain yourself one hundred percent. You are always asking somebody else to do something for you, on a larger scale or on a smaller scale. But if you look very closely at what you are doing, it becomes unreasonable.

Sometimes, if he is brave enough, your husband might say to you: "Isn't there some blame on your side as well? Mightn't you also have to join in and do something about it?" Or if your wife is brave enough, she will tell you that the situation might have something to do with both of you. If your spouse is somewhat timid and intelligent, he might say, "Both of us are to blame." But nobody says, "It is *you* who has to change." Whenever anybody does say, "It's your problem, not anybody else's," you don't like it at all. We have a problem with relative bodhichitta here.

The text says: "Drive all blames into one." The reason you have to do that is because you have been cherishing yourself so much, even at the cost of sacrificing somebody else's life. You have been cherishing yourself, holding yourself so dearly. Although sometimes you might say that you don't like yourself, even then in your heart of hearts you know that you like yourself so much that you're willing to throw everybody else down the drain, down the gutter. You are really willing to do that. You are willing to let somebody sacrifice his life, give himself away for you. And who are you, anyway? So the point is that all blames should be driven into oneself. This slogan is the first slogan connected with viewing your whole life as part of the path of relative bodhichitta.

This slogan does not mean you should not speak up. If you see something that is obviously destructive to everybody, you should speak out. But you can speak out in the form of driving all blames into yourself. The question is how to present it to the authorities. Usually you come at them in an aggressive, traditionally American way. You have been trained to speak for yourself and for others in the democratic style of the "lord of speech." You come out with placards and complaints: "We don't like this." But that only solidifies the authorities even more. There could be a much better way of approaching the whole thing, a more intelligent way. You could say, "Maybe it's my problem, but personally I find that this water doesn't taste good." You and your friends could say, "We don't feel good about drinking this water." It could be very simple and straightforward. You don't have to go through the whole legal trip. You don't have to use the "lord of speech" approach of making public declarations of all kinds, "Freedom for all mankind!" or anything like that. Maybe you could even bring along your dog or your cat. I think the whole thing could be done very gently.

Obviously, there are social problems, but the way to approach that is not as "I—a rightful political entity," or as "me—one of the important people in society." Democracy is built on the attitude that I speak out for myself, the invincible me. I speak for democracy. I would like to get my own rights, and I also speak for others' rights as well. Therefore, we don't want to have this water. But that approach doesn't work. The point is that people's experience of themselves could be gathered together, rather than just having a rally. That is what you do in sitting practice.

In an extreme case, if I happened to find myself in the central head-quarters where they push the button that could blow up the planet, I would kill the person who was going to push the button for the bomb right away and without any hesitation. I would take delight in it! But that is slightly different from what we are talking about. In that case, you are dealing with the threshold of the power of society altogether. In this case, we are simply talking about how we can collectively smooth out this world, so that it could become an enlightened society. Creating an enlightened society requires general cultivation of that nature.

13

*Be grateful to everyone.**

This slogan also is dealing with *kündzop*, or conventional reality. That is to say, without this world we cannot attain enlightenment, there would be no journey. By rejecting the world, we would be rejecting the ground and rejecting the path. All our past history and all our neurosis is related with others in some sense. All of our experiences are based on others, basically. As long as we have a sense of practice, some realization that we are treading on the path, every one of those little details that are seemingly obstacles to us becomes an essential part of the path. Without them we cannot attain anything at all—we have no feedback, we have nothing to work with, absolutely nothing to work with.

So in a sense all the things taking place around our world, all the ir-ritations and all the problems, are crucial. Without others we cannot at-

---

*A more literal translation of this slogan is "Contemplate the great kindness of everyone."

tain enlightenment—in fact, we cannot even tread on the path. In other words, we could say that if there is no noise outside during our sitting meditation, we cannot develop mindfulness. If we do not have aches and pains in our body, we cannot attain mindfulness, we cannot actually meditate. If everything were lovey-dovey and jellyfishlike, there would be nothing to work with. Everything would be completely blank. Because of all these textures around us, we are enriched. Therefore, we can sit and practice and meditate. We have a reference point—encouragement, discouragement, or whatever. Everything is related to the path.

The idea of this particular teaching is actually to give our blood and flesh to others. "If you want me, take me, possess me, kidnap me, control me—go ahead, do it. Take me. I'm at your service. You could bounce on me, shit on me, cut me into pieces or anything you want. Without your help I would not have any way to work with my journey at all." That is a very, very powerful thing. In fact, one of the interesting sayings of Lang-ri Thangpa, one of the Kadampa teachers, was: "I realize that all mistakes belong to me and all virtues belong to others, so I cannot really blame anybody except myself."

There is a little phrase which might be good to memorize. In Tibet we used to stick it on our door handles and things like that. The saying goes: "Profit and victory to others; loss and defeat to myself." That sounds terribly self-flagellating if you look at it the wrong way. In particular, the popular idea of Catholicism is to blame everything on oneself as an ultimate guilt concept. But in this case, we are not talking about guilt or that we did something terribly wrong. It is seeing things as they are. By "profit and victory," we mean anything that encourages us to walk on the path of dharma—that is created by the world. Yet at the same time we are filled with loss and defeat all the time—that is ours. We are not supposed to sulk on that particular point, but we are supposed to take pride in that. It is a fantastic idea that we are actually, finally fearless persons—that profit is others' and loss is ours. That is great, fantastic! We may not find that to be so when it is early morning and we have just woken up and feel rather feeble; although at the end of the day, when we have had a few drinks and our belly is filled and we are relatively comfortable, we might feel that way. But fundamentally it is true.

These statements are not based on guilt or punishment, like the Jewish idea of *oy vey*. But it is actually true that a lot of things that we tend to blame others for are our own doing—otherwise we wouldn't get in trouble. How come somebody else doesn't get in trouble and we do get in trouble? What causes that? It must be something happening to us, obviously. We can write our case history and employ our own lawyer to prove that we are right and somebody else is wrong—but that is also trouble we have to go through. It is all trouble, problems. And trying to prove our case history somehow doesn't work. In any case, hiring a lawyer to attain enlightenment is not done. It is not possible. Buddha did not have a lawyer himself.

The slogan "Be grateful to everyone" follows automatically once we drive all blames into one. We have a feeling that if others didn't exist to hassle us, we couldn't drive all blames into ourselves at all. All sentient beings, all the people in the world, or most of them, have a problem in dealing with "myself." Without others, we would have no chance at all to develop beyond ego. So the idea here is to feel grateful that others are presenting us with tremendous obstacles—even threats or challenges. The point is to appreciate that. Without them, we could not follow the path at all.

Walking on the path of the dharma is connected with dealing with our neurosis. But if there were no neuros-*ees*, we couldn't develop any neuros-*is*. Therefore, we should feel very grateful to such persons. They are actually the ones who are pushing us onto the path of dharma. I will tell you a little story about Atisha, who is the source of these teachings. Atisha was invited to teach in Tibet, and he had heard that the Tibetans were very kind, gentle, hospitable people. So he decided that he should take along with him one object of practice—his attendant, a Bengali servant who was very short-tempered. Since the Tibetans were so kind and good, Atisha took his servant along so that he could practice lojong on him. Interestingly enough, he said later on that he needn't have brought this person, as the Tibetans were not as good as he had heard.

If someone hurts you, you should be thankful to them for giving you the opportunity to practice. But you do not have to expose yourself to be hurt, that would be some sort of martyrdom. You don't have to ask to be hurt, but when you come up with such a situation, then all the things we discussed apply. It is not that you have to stage the whole thing. Instead, somebody will blame you and then you will think, "It is mine." You don't have to avoid such situations and you don't have to cultivate them. You just lead your life, being very sane, and you don't hurt anybody else. But if anybody happens to hurt you, then you know what to do. It is very simple. We are not talking about deliberately jumping on a sword. That would be a misunderstanding. Instead you are making a close relationship with the person who is hurting you.

At a further level of development it may be possible to stop an attacker by force to prevent him from having the karma of having injured you. But that is a very high level of sympathy. For instance, there is a story about a Tibetan teacher who was ambushed by his enemies, who were going to kill him on his way to teaching a seminary. He pulled out his dagger and said, "This is the tooth of a tiger," and he stabbed the chief, killing him on the spot. Everybody was so shocked, they let him go. That is an entirely different approach. I think it would be too dangerous for us to go as far as that. As long as you know what you are doing, it is okay, but that sort of approach escalates the warfare.

"Loss and defeat" is not really pain in the fundamental sense, it is just a game. It is that you did not get what you wanted, so you feel somewhat irritated, the little things that go through our life always. It has nothing to do with real pain. We do not always get what we want and we are always frustrated with that. We are resentful toward something or somebody or even toward ourselves if we expend our money or if we run into somebody's car or anything of that nature. It is not really pain, it is just hassle.

This whole approach is dealing with all kinds of hassles and transmuting them and working with them as a workable journey toward enlightenment. We are not talking about fundamental pain. I think one of the problems we have, particularly in the Occidental mentality, is that we make too much of a big deal of the whole thing. We complicate the whole thing unnecessarily, and we have no idea how to play games properly. It is not a big deal, it is an exchange. You are finally putting your name on the dotted line. It is a lighthearted situation—including death. Keep that in mind. Make a slogan out of that. Whatever takes place, you do not take all that seriously. Whatever comes up, you do not regard as the ultimate, final problem, but as a temporary flare-up that comes and goes.

This obviously needs a lot of understanding and training. A person cannot practice this without preplanning the journey and having worked with his or her state of mind. There is also a need for some understanding of the shunyata experience, basically speaking. There is no ground at all to begin with, so anything that takes place in the groundlessness becomes workable. Those things are actually very powerful—they used to be, anyway. When I was a teenager it really turned me on a great deal. It is so direct and very simple and helpful—particularly when you are facing hassles.

14

Seeing confusion as the four kayas
Is unsurpassable shunyata protection.

In the slogan "Seeing confusion as the four kayas / Is unsurpassable shunyata protection," the basic question is whom to protect, what to protect. All sorts of other questions are involved as well, but basically we are talking about having an understanding or realization of the way we perceive things as they are.

In perception, first there will be a sense of waiting or openness. There may be uncertainty as to how to perceive things, not knowing how to make a particular situation graspable. Then we have a clear idea of how to organize things. Thirdly, we begin to make a relationship between the two. And finally we have a total experience of the whole. That makes four states of mind that we go through, four stages of mind or mental process. These four processes are related with the four kayas: *dharmakaya, sambhogakaya, nirmanakaya,* and *svabhavikakaya.*

The dharmakaya nature of our reaction to the world is usually uncertain, bewildered. Strategies are not yet formed, planning is not completely organized—it is just a sense of basic openness. The nirmanakaya aspect is the second stage of this process. At this point there is some kind of clarity in which we have a basic grasp of the situation generally. And in order to make a link between the uncertainty or openness and the clarity, we need sambhogakaya, which bridges the gap between the two and joins them together. So the dharmakaya and the nirmanakaya are joined together by means of the sambhogakaya. According to this particular tradition, that is the realistic way of looking at things.[1]

Svabhavikakaya is understanding the whole thing, total panoramic experience. When we begin to flash our mind to an object, when we have a grasp of it, when we begin to realize some kind of link between the kayas—that totality is what is known as svabhavikakaya.

The svabhavikakaya is a general state of existence, and that state of mind also contains what is known as transcending birth, cessation, and dwelling. Transcending birth means that thought process does not come up. There is no such thing as the birth of a mind or the birth of a thought taking place in our state of being at all, there is just simply existing and opening. Transcending cessation means that no thoughts actually subside, unless they are replaced or overlapped by something else. And transcending dwelling means that thoughts do not dwell anywhere, although there is some kind of occasional something. So the idea of svabhavikakaya is seeing beyond the birth, subsiding, and dwelling of the thought process.

The reason that the four kayas—dharmakaya, sambhogakaya, nirmanakaya, and svabhavikakaya—become a great protection is that we begin to realize the way our mind functions, our state of being. We realize that whatever comes up in our mind is always subject to that flow, that particular case history, that nature. Sudden pain, sudden anger, sudden aggression, sudden passion—whatever might arise always follows the same procedure, so to speak, the same process. Everything is always in accordance with the four kayas. Although we might not regard our own mind as all that transcendent and enlightened or awake, its pattern is still that of the four kaya principles. So the nature of everything is nowness. Thoughts just emerge: you cannot watch their birth, they are just there. They die, they just [Vidyadhara snaps fingers]. They don't dwell, they just [Vidyadhara snaps fingers again]. The whole thing is a natural process.

This slogan might seem slightly obscure, but it has to do with the absolute bodhichitta concept of understanding your mind by studying and watching yourself and by practicing shamatha and vipashyana. By practicing those disciplines, you begin to realize that the essence of your mind is empty, that the nature of your mind is light and clear, and that the expression or manifestation of your mind is active. That realization can only come about when you are sitting on the cushion. Only on the cushion can you see that your mind has no origin. There is no place from which thoughts arise, as far as you can judge by looking at them. You also have no idea where your thoughts go. Thoughts just come and they just vanish, disappear. Furthermore, you also have no idea where your thoughts dwell—particularly when you have developed a basic sense of mindfulness and awareness.

As you continue to practice mindfulness and awareness, the seeming confusion and chaos in your mind begin to seem absurd. You begin to realize that your thoughts have no real birthplace, no origin, they just pop up as dharmakaya. They are unborn. And your thoughts don't go anywhere, they are unceasing. Therefore, your mind is seen as sambhogakaya. And furthermore, no activities are really happening in your mind, so the notion that your mind can dwell on anything also begins to seem absurd, because there is nothing to dwell on. Therefore, your mind is seen as nirmanakaya. Putting the whole thing together, there is no birth, no cessation, and no acting or dwelling at all—therefore, your mind is seen as svabhavikakaya. The point is not to make your mind a blank. It is just that as a result of supermindfulness and superawareness, you begin to see that nothing is actually happening—although at the same time you think that lots of things are happening.

Realizing that the confusion and the chaos in your mind have no origin, no cessation, and nowhere to dwell is the best protection. Shunyata is the best protection because it cuts the solidity of your beliefs. "I have my solid thought" or "This is my grand thought" or "My thought is so cute" or "In my thoughts I visualize a grand whatever" or "The star men came down and talked to me" or "Genghis Khan is present in my mind" or "Jesus Christ himself manifested in my mind" or "I have thought of a tremendous scheme a for how to build a city, or how to write a tremendous musical comedy, or how to conquer the world"—it could be anything, from that level down to: "How am I going to earn my living after this?" or "What is the best way for me to sharpen my personality so that I will be visible in the world?" or "How I hate my problems!" All of those schemes and thoughts and ideas are empty! If you look behind their backs, it is like looking at a mask. If you look behind a mask, you see that it is hollow. There may be a few holes for the nostrils and the mouth—but if you look behind it, it doesn't look like a face anymore, it is just junk with holes in it. Realizing that is your best protection. You realize that you are no longer the greatest artist at all, that you are not any of your big ideas. You realize that you are just authoring absurd, nonexistent things. That is the best protection for cutting confusion.

This slogan is related with the idea of carrying everything onto the path at the absolute bodhichitta level. It is very tricky. There is some possibility that when you hear that if you just simply meditate on the four kayas, everything is going to be protected, you may think that your kid is going to be protected, your brothers and sisters, your property and your motorcars. But this protection is not quite at that level; it is shunyata protection, which is that you no longer have anywhere to dwell, you are suspended in shunyata. It is a very clever way of approaching the whole thing. You are not talking about egolessness here, you are trying to work out your protection. But you might find yourself being egoless and realizing that there is nothing to protect. So your protection is groundlessness. It is a very clinical approach in some sense. There can be no germs around if you have no ground on which to collect germs.

The idea of the four kayas is not particularly tantric, it is mahayanist high thinking. The kayas appear in the third turning of the wheel of the dharma in the *Uttaratantra* of Maitreya[2] and in the *Diamond Sutra*.[3] So this is not particularly a tantric idea. But at the same time, it is tantric in some sense. If I may say so, the idea of dealing with *döns* and with the protectors is highly influenced by tantra. [See the upcoming slogan, "Four practices are the best of methods."] The whole thing is based on mahayana principles, but there is an undercurrent of techniques that are borrowed from the vajrayana. So the understanding is presented from the mahayana viewpoint, but the techniques are tantric.

15

Four practices are the best of methods.

This slogan is a rather difficult one, actually, but it makes a lot of sense. It refers to special activities, or anecdotes, for how to go about your daily life, translated as "best of methods." These best methods consist of four categories: accumulating merits, laying down evil deeds, offering to the döns, and offering to the *dharmapalas*.

Accumulating Merit

The first application is accumulating merit, not in the sense that we are accumulating anything for our own ego trip, but from the point of view of trying to relate with what is sacred or holy. We are making a connection with sacred areas of reality: the very idea of the teachings, or dharma, and the existence of basic sanity, which is represented by works of art, images, statues, paintings, books, all kinds of symbols and all kind of colors. We associate ourselves with that kind of thing. Creating merit is working with such situations and putting in as much of our effort and energy as we can. A sense of veneration becomes very important.

The accumulation of merit is also based on complete trust in the *three types of encouragement*. These three are not slogans; they are lines of encouragement for the slogans, so to speak. The three lines of encouragemerit are:

> Grant your blessing if it is better for me to be sick.
> Grant your blessing if it is better for me to survive.
> Grant your blessing if it is better for me to be dead.

That is the ultimate idea of creating merit. That is to say, we cannot have a succession of merit completely filling the whole area absolutely. Before we beg, our begging bowl has to be emptied; otherwise nobody will give us anything. In order to receive something, there first has to be a sense of openness, giving, surrendering. It is not being concerned with yourself, it is simply letting things be. Whatever comes up, be grateful to it. It is not that you are not talking to anybody; instead it is like saying, "Let the rain fall," or "Let the earth shake." It is a magical word, simply. Something actually might happen when you do that, but you are not talking to anybody in particular. I don't know how I can say that linguistically: "Grant your blessings," or "Just let it happen."

Traditionally one creates merit by creating statues and stupas and by making offerings to the *sangha*—donating our money and encouraging that kind of establishment. But we are not only surrendering our green energy. We are also trying to let go of our possessiveness altogether. For instance, if it is better for us to get sick, we let it be so. "Please let that be our blessing."

We might regard this approach as that of a very naive person who will go along with absolutely anything all the time. But in this case, the approach has to be an extremely intelligent one which lets us go ahead and open ourselves completely to the situation. That seems to be a very important point—that we cannot just have blind faith. We have to have the intelligent faith of letting so of our holding back. Holding back creates a kind of business mentality: "If I don't get this, then I have to sue the Buddha, the dharma, and the sangha—metaphorically, realistically, or whatever. If I don't get my money's worth in return, then I have been cheated." But in this case it is not so much tit for tat, but letting things be in their own way: "Whatever has happened, I would like to let go of this problem of holding back." It is very simple. It is extremely simple and realistic. That is precisely what is meant by creating or accumulating merit.

We cannot accumulate merit if we have a macho sense of pride and arrogance that we already have enough truth and virtue collected and now we are going to collect some more. The person who collects merit has to be humble and willing to give rather than being willing to collect. The more a person is willing to give, that much more effective, in some sense, is the accumulation of merit. That is why there are those three subslogans or reminders. We could actually call them incantations, that might be a better word. The slogans themselves are reminders; so these incantations are reminders for the reminders.

When we talk about merit, we are not talking about collecting something for your ego but about the basic twist of how to punish your ego. The logic is that you always want pleasure, but what you get is always pain. Why does that happen? It happens because the very act of seeking pleasure brings pain. You always get a bad deal—all the time. You get a bad deal because you started at the wrong end of the stick.

The point of this practice or application is that you have to sacrifice something rather than purely yearning for pleasure. You have to start at the right end of the stick from the very beginning. In order to do that, you have to refrain from evil actions and cultivate virtuous actions. In order to do that, you have to block out hope and fear altogether so you do not hope to gain anything from your practice and you are not particularly fearful of bad results.

Whatever happens, let it happen—you are not particularly looking for pleasure or pain. As the supplications that go along with this particular practice say: "If it is better for me to be dead, let me be dead; if it is better for me to be alive, let me be alive. If it is better for me to have pleasure, let me have pleasure; if it is better for me to have pain, let me have pain." It is a very direct approach, like diving into an ice-cold swimming pool in the middle of winter. If that is what is best for your constitution, go ahead and do it. It is the idea of having a direct link with reality, very simple, without any scheming at all. In particular, if there is any desire or any fear, you act in the opposite way: you jump into your fear and you refrain from your desire. It is the same approach as taking on other people's pain and giving your pleasure to them. It should no longer be any surprise to you that we have such a strange way of dealing with the whole thing—but it usually works. We could almost say that it works one hundred percent, but I'm not sure about two hundred percent.

Laying Down Evil Deeds

The second of the four practices is laying down your evil deeds or neurotic crimes. As a result of accumulating merit, because you have learned to block out hope and fear altogether, you have developed a sense of gentleness and sanity. Having done so, the basic idea of laying down evil actions is psychological: you look back and you say, "Good heavens! I have been so stupid, and I didn't even realize it!" Such an attitude develops because you have already, at least somewhat, reached a certain level of sophistication. When you look back, you begin to see how sloppy and how embarrassing you have been. The reason you didn't notice it before is because of stupidity of some kind. So the point is to look back and realize what you have been doing and not make the same mistake all over again. I think that is quite straightforward.

We have translated the Tibetan term *dikpa* as "evil deeds" or "neurotic crimes" rather than "sin."[4] The word *sin* has all kinds of connotations. Particularly in the world of dead or living Christendom, and in theistic traditions generally, it is all-pervasive. *Dikpa* literally means "sin," but not in the same way as we refer to it in the Christian or Judaic traditions. "Neurotic crimes" has psychological implications rather than being purely ethical. When neurosis begins to surge up, you begin to go along with that process and you begin to do something funny. It may seem fantastic and far out, but it results in frivolity from that point of view. So neurosis is the backbone and frivolity is the activities.

The crime itself can end up as all kinds of crimes and destruction. What we are discussing is that basic principle of neurosis which creates all kinds of frivolous activities. We are confessing that. We are not talking about confession as going to a priest in a little box saying, "Father, I did a terrible thing yesterday, what should I do for that?" And the father would say, "Say this twenty times and we could let you go." Then you can come back next time saying the same thing and he might say, "You have been bad in the past, so this time you should say it fifty times, your father is keeping a record of you." Everything depends on red tape from that point of view. But in this case it is a more personal situation. In the Buddhist style of confession, shall we say, there is no church or particular building to go into to confess your evil deeds or neurotic crimes. There is a fourfold style of doing the whole thing, which is not so much confession as relieving the sin or the neurotic crimes.

The first step is getting tired of one's own neurosis. That is the first important thing. If you were not tired of doing the same thing again and again—all the time—if you were thriving on it, you probably would not have a chance to do anything with it. But once you begin to get tired of it, you say: "I shouldn't have done that," or "Here I go again," or "I should have known better," or "I don't feel so good." These are the sort of remarks you make, particularly when you wake up in the morning with a heavy hangover. That's good, that is the sign that you can actually confess your neurotic crimes. You come back and tell what you did last night or yesterday or what you've done previously. All these things are so embarrassing, it's terrible. You feel like not getting out of your bed. You don't want to go outside the door or face the world.

That real feeling of total embarrassment, that totally shitty feeling, for lack of a better word, that sense that your whole gut is rotten, is the first step. That sense of regret is not purely social regret—it is personal regret. And that shameful feeling begins to creep through our marrow into our bones and our hairs. The sunshine coming through the windows begins to mock us, too. It is that kind of thing. That is the first step. And having it is regarded as a very healthy direction toward the second.

The second step is to refrain from that or to repent. "From this time onward I am not going to do it. I am going to hold off on what I have been doing." Repentance usually takes place in us when we begin to feel that we have done such a shitty job previously: "Do I still want to do it? Maybe it is fun, but it is still better not to do it." As we think more and more about it, it does not seem to be a hot idea to do it again. So there is a sense of refraining from it, preventing doing it again. That is the second step to confessing or relieving our evil deeds or neurotic crimes.

The third step is taking refuge. We realize that having done such things already, they are not particularly subject to one person's forgiveness. This is a difference from the Christian tradition, seemingly. Nobody can wipe out your neurosis by saying, "I forgive you." Quite possibly the person you forgave would not attack *you* again, but he or she might kill somebody else. From that point of view, unless the whole crime has completely subsided, forgiving does not help. It not only does not help, it may even encourage you to do more sinning. From the Buddhist approach, the fact that a person has already wiped out your neurotic crimes, has created a good relationship with you, and understands and forgives you inspires you to commit further crimes. So in this case, forgiveness means that one has to give oneself up altogether. The criminal has to give up altogether rather than the crime being forgiven.

Actions alone are not particularly a big deal; the basic factors which a person puts into the act of committing a crime are more important. People have begun to realize this, even in the modern world. We have begun to realize that we have to reform people in the jails and give them further training so that they do not go back to their crimes. Often people simply get free board and lodging, and once their sentences are over they could have a good time because they have served their sentence, they are forgiven, and everything is fine. If they are hungry again and without any food, money, or shelter, they could come back. So the idea of reformation is very tricky. According to history, apparently Buddhists never had jails, not even Emperor Ashoka. He was the first person who denounced having jails.

The idea of taking refuge is completely surrendering. Complete surrendering is based on the notion that you have to give up the criminal rather than that the crime should be forgiven. That is the idea of taking refuge in the Buddha as the example, in the dharma as the path, and in the sangha as companionship—giving up oneself, giving up one's stronghold.

The fourth step is a further completing of that surrendering process. At this point a person is surrendering, giving, and opening completely. A person should actually engage in a supplication of preventing hope and fear. That is very important. "If hope is too hopeful, may I not be too hopeful. If fear is too fearful, may I not be too fearful." Transcending both hope and fear, you begin to develop a sense of confidence that you could go through the whole thing. That is the power of activity to relieve one's evil deeds.

So the first step is a sense of disgust with what you have done. The second one is refraining from it. The third is that, understanding that, you begin to take refuge in the Buddha, dharma, and sangha—offering your neurosis. Having offered your neurosis or taken refuge, you begin to commit yourself as a traveler on the path rather than as any big deal or moneymaker on the path. All those processes somehow connect together. And finally there is no hope and no fear: "If there is hope, let our hope subside; if there is any fear, may our fear subside as well." That is the fourth step.

Offering to the Döns

Number three is traditionally called "feeding the ghosts." It refers to those ghosts who create sickness, misfortune, or anything like that, called *döns* in Tibetan. The idea is to tell them: "I feel so grateful that you have caused me harm in the past, and I would like to invite you to come back again and again to do the same thing to me. I feel so grateful that you have woken me up from my sleepiness, my slothfulness. At least when I had my attack of flu, I felt much different from my usual laziness and stupidity, my usual wallowing in pleasure." You ask them to wake you up as much as they can. Whenever any difficult situation comes along, you begin to feel grateful. At this point you regard anything that can wake you up as best. You regard anything that provides you with the opportunity for mindfulness or awareness, anything that shocks you, as best, rather than always trying to ward off any problems.

Traditionally one offers the ghosts *torma*, or food. *Torma* is a Tibetan word meaning "offering cake." If you have watched a Tibetan ceremony, you may have seen funny little cakes carved out of butter and dough. Those are called torma. They represent the idea of a gift or token. A similar concept in the West is the birthday cake, which is designed and planned in a certain way, with artwork on it and completely decorated. So we give offerings to those who create harm to us, which literally means those who are creating an evil influence on us.

The first practice, the confession of sins, is just natural tiredness of one's continual neurosis. One's neurosis is not particularly a landmark, it is just a natural thing which comes up, not a big attack. But a dön is a big attack or sudden earthshaking situation which makes you think twice. A sudden incident hits you and suddenly things begin to happen to you. So something remarkable is taking place. The first one is just sort of a camel's hump rather than a sheer drop. It is simply relating with ups and downs, pains. The second application talks about getting tired of your particular problems. You have a sense of your neurosis going on all the time. It is like somebody with a migraine headache: it keeps coming up, again and again. You are tired of that. You are tired of doing the same things again and again. The third practice or application says that we should give torma to those who harm us, the döns.

Döns are very abrupt, very direct. Everything is going smoothly, and suddenly an attack takes place: your grandmother has disinherited you, or there is a shift of luck. Döns usually attack much more suddenly; they possess you immediately. *Possession* is actually the closest word for dön. They are equated with possession because they attack you suddenly and they attack you by surprise. Suddenly you are in a terribly bad mood even though everything is okay.

This subject is a very complicated one, actually. We are not just talking about trying to feed somebody who spooks us, those little fairies who might turn against us: "Let us feed them some little thingies and they might go away." It is connected with the whole Tibetan concept of dön, which comes from the Pön tradition[5] but also seems to be applicable to the Buddhist tradition. The word *dön* means a sense or experience of something existing around us that suddenly makes us unreasonably fearful, unreasonably angry and aggressive, unreasonably horny and passionate, or unreasonably mean. Situations of that kind occur to us throughout our life. There is some kind of flu or fever that goes on all the time in our life, that possesses us. Without any reason we are suddenly terrified. Without any reason we are so angry and uptight. Without any reason we are so lustful. Without any reason we are suddenly so proud. It is a neurotic attack of some kind, which is called a dön. If we approach that from an external point of view, certain phenomena make us do that. To extend that logic, we could say that such spirits exist outside us: "The ghost of Washington hit us, so we are inspired to run for the presidency," or whatever.

That feeling of some hidden neurosis which keeps popping up all the time is called dön. It happens to us all the time. Suddenly we break into tears, for absolutely no reason. We cry and cry and cry and break down completely. And at a certain point we would like to destroy the whole world and kick everybody out. We would like to destroy our house. If we have a wife or children, we could knock them out as well. We go to extremes, of course. And sometimes the dön doesn't go along with that. As we go along with what we have started, the dön doesn't want to be a complaint, so it pulls back. We go ahead with our fists extended in midair on the way to our wife's eyes—and suddenly there is nobody to encourage us, so our hands just drop down.

Döns are like some kind of flu that takes us over and is usually unpredictable. It happens to us all the time, sometimes to a lesser extent and sometimes to a greater extent. The idea is to understand and realize that such things are taking place in us, that neurotic processes are beginning to pop up in us. We can be thankful for that. We could say that it is great that it takes place: "It is great that you actually snatched back the debt I owe you, that you confiscated the debt I owe you. Please come back and do the same thing again and again. Please come back and do so." We do not regard the whole thing as playing trick or treat, that if we give them enough, they are going to go away—they come back again.

And we should invite them back, the ups and downs of those sudden attacks of neurosis. It is quite dangerous: wives might be afraid of getting black eyes again and again, and husbands might have fears of being unable to enter their home and have a good dinner. But it is still important to invite them again and again, to realize their possibilities. We are not going to get rid of them. We are going to have to acknowledge that and be thankful for what has happened. Usually such an upsurge coincides with a physical weakness of some kind, as if we were just about to catch the flu or a cold.

Sometimes you are careless. You don't eat the right food and you go out without a coat and you catch cold. Or you do not watch your step and you slip and break your disk or you break your rib. Whenever there is a little gap, döns could slip in, in the same way that we catch cold. Things always happen that way. You might have complete control of the whole thing, but on the other hand, the problems have complete control also, which creates a loss of mindfulness. So a lot of döns can attack you. The idea is that if you are completely working with mindfulness twenty-four hours a day you do not have döns, you do not have a flu, you do not have a cold. But once you are not at that level, you have all kinds of things happening. You have to face that fact. It could be said that at the level of mindfulness, such problems can be avoided absolutely. That is an advertisement for being mindful.

You welcome such attacks when you lose your mindfulness. They are reminders and you are grateful because they tell you how much you are being unmindful. They are always welcome: "Don't go, please come back." But at the same time, you continue with your mindfulness. It is the same as working with your teacher. You don't try to avoid the teacher all the time. If you are okay, you will always have some kind of reference point to the teacher. But at some point the teacher might shout at you, "Boo!" and you still have to work with it. The reason why you welcome them is that their presence means something to you in terms of your direction, what's going on.

Usually what happens with us is that we have a schedule and everything is going along smoothly and ideally, hunky-dory, everything is fine and nothing is problematic—and one day we are suddenly uptight, one day we are so down. Everything is smooth and ordinary, and then there are those ups and downs, those little puncturing situations in our lives. Little leaks, little upsurges take place all the time. The idea is to feed those forces with torma.

If we are trying to do that literally, probably we will still have the same fits all the time. The idea of offering torma is somewhat symbolic in this case. I don't think we can get rid of our ups and downs by giving them some little Tibetan offerings. That would be far-fetched. Forgive me, but that is true, actually. It needs more of a gesture than that. If we have a real feeling about offering something which represents our existence and put it out as an expression or demonstration of our opening and giving up, that could be okay. But that comes at a higher level. In particular, people in this environment are not trained in that kind of ritualistic world, so people have very little feelings about such things. Ritualism becomes more a superstition than a sacred ceremony. That has become problematic. Few people have experienced anything of that nature and had it become meaningful. It means that we actually have to commit ourselves rather than just having somebody sprinkling water on us, trying to make us feel good and happy. We have not experienced the depth of ritualism to the extent that we could actually put out cakes for the döns so that they will not attack us again. In order to do that we need further suitability of our own state of being as well as a sense of immense sanity. So I would not like to suggest that you put out substitute doggy bags for anybody—although it might be good for the local dogs and cats.

Offering to the Dharmapalas

Number four is asking the *dharmapalas*, or "protectors of the teachings," to help you in your practice. This is not quite the same as praying to your patron saint, asking him to make sure you can cross the river safely. Let me just give you a very ordinary, basic idea of this. You have your root guru, your teacher, who guides you and blesses you, so that you could become a worthy student. At a lower level, you have protectors of the teachings, who will push you back to your discipline if you stray into any problems. They are sort of like shepherds: if one sheep decides to run away, the shepherd drives it back into the corral. You know that if you stray, the protectors will teach you how to come back. They will give you all sorts of messages. For instance, when you are in the middle of a tremendous fit of anger and aggression and you have become a cormpletely nondharmic person, you might slam the door and catch your finger in it. That teaches you something. It is the principle of corraling you back to the world where you belong. If you have the slightest temptation to step out of the dharmic world, the protectors will herd you back—*hurl* you back—to that world. That is the meaning of asking the dharmapalas, or the protectors, to help you in your practice.

The dharmapalas represent our basic awareness, which is not so much absorbed in the meditative state of being but which takes place or takes care of us during the postmeditation experience. That is why traditionally we have chanting taking place toward the end of the day, it is time to go to sleep or eat dinner, and when it is time to wake up in the morning. The idea is that from morning to evening, our life is controlled or secured purely by practice and learning all the time. So our life is sacred.

Toward the end of our day, quite possibly we have possibilities of taking a break from sacred activity and meditative activity. At that time, quite possibly all kinds of neurosis beyond measure could attack us. So that is the most dangerous time. The darkness is connected with evil in some sense, not as the Christian concept of Satan, particularly, but evil as some kind of hidden neurosis which might be indulged and which thereby might create obstacles to realization. Moreover, our practice of meditation may be relaxed—so in order not to create a complete break from sitting practice or discipline, in order to continue, we ask these protectors of the dharma to work with us. They are no more than ourselves. They are our expression of intelligence or of mind, which happens constantly. And their particular job is to destroy any kind of violence or confusion which takes place in us.

Usually confusion is connected with aggression a great deal. It is *adharma* or antidharma. Dharma does not have a sense of aggression; it is just simple truth. But truth can be diverted or challenged or relocated by all kinds of conceptual ideas. Truth can be cut into pieces by one's own individual aggression. There is also the possibility that our individual aggression is regarded not as dirty aggression but as very polite aggression, smeared with honey and milk. Such aggression is known as an ego trip, and it needs to be cut through.

According to this particular application, it is very necessary to work with that kind of energy. To do so we have developed all kinds of chants here in the West as well as in Tibet. We have whole huge *sadhanas* of various *mahakalas* whose job it is to cut through blood-thirsty subconscious gossip which does not allow any sense of openness and simplicity and peace or gentleness. The idea is to relate with gentleness at this point. And in order to bring gentleness into effect, so to speak, we have to cut through aggression at the same time. Otherwise, there would be no gentleness. Traditional chants represent the idea that anybody who has violated the gentleness has to be cut through by means of gentleness. When gentleness becomes so harsh, it could become very powerful and cut right through. By cutting through, it creates further gentleness. It is like when a doctor says that it is not going to hurt you, it is just going to be a little prick. One little prick and you are cured. It is that kind of idea.

A further understanding of the mahakalas or the dharmapalas that we are inviting is connected with the presentation of the teachings and how it can be handled properly in an individual's mind. That is one of our biggest concerns—or at least *my* biggest concern. If the teachings are not properly presented or are presented in the wrong way or in a somewhat cowardly way—if true teaching has not been presented, we all could be struck down by that. So we are asking the protectors to give us help and feedback through teachings, through bankruptcies, through organizational mishaps, through being millionaires, or through work in general. It is all included. We are taking a lot of chances here. We are not physically taking chances as much as we are taking spiritual chances. That seems to be the basic point of what we are doing. And giving offerings to the dharmapalas is what we have been told to do according to this commentary of Jamgön Kongtrül.

16

Whatever you meet unexpectedly, join with meditation.

There are three sets of slogans connected with how to carry everyday occurrences into practice on the path. The first set is connected with relative bodhichitta and includes the slogans "Drive all blames into one" and "Be grateful to everyone." The second set is connected with absolute bodhichitta and comprises the slogan "Seeing confusion as the four kayas / Is unsurpassable shunyata protection." The third set is the special activities connected with following the path. The headline slogan for that is "Four practices are the best of methods." And having discussed those three categories, there is a tail end, which is this slogan "Whatever you meet unexpectedly, join with meditation." It is not necessarily the least, but it is the last. It is the last slogan of the third point of mind training, which is concerned with bringing your experience onto the path properly, and it is actually a very interesting one.

In this slogan, the word *join* has the feeling of putting together butter and bread. You put together or join situations with meditation, or with shamatha-vipashyana. The idea is that whatever comes up is not a sudden threat or an encouragement or any of that bullshit. Instead it simply goes along with one's discipline, one's awareness of compassion. If somebody hits you in the face, that's fine. Or if somebody decides to steal your bottle of Coke, that's fine too. This is somewhat naive, in a way, but at the same time it is very powerful.

Generally speaking, Western audiences have a problem with this kind of thing. It sounds love-and-lighty, like the hippie ethic in which "Everything is going to be okay. Everybody is everybody's property, everything is everybody's property. You can share anything with anybody. Don't lay ego trips on things." But this is something more than that. It is not love-and-light. It is simply to be open and precise, and to know your territory at the same time. You are going to relate with your own neurosis rather than expanding that neurosis to others.

"Whatever you meet" could be either a pleasurable or a painful situation—but it always comes in the form of a surprise. You think that you have settled your affairs properly: you have your little apartment and you are settled in New York City; your friends come around, and everything is okay; business is fine. Suddenly, out of nowhere, you realize that you have run out of money! Or, for that matter, your boyfriend or your girlfriend is giving you up. Or the floor of your apartment is falling down. Even simple situations could come as quite a surprise: you are in the middle of peaceful, calm sitting practice, everything is fine— and then somebody says, "Fuck you!" An insult out of nowhere. On the other hand, maybe somebody says, "I think you're a fantastic person," or you suddenly inherit a million dollars just as you are fixing up your apartment which is falling apart. The surprise could go both ways.

"Whatever you meet" refers to any sudden occurrence like that. That is why the slogan says that whatever you meet, any situation you come across, should be joined immediately with meditation. Whatever shakes you should without delay, right away, be incorporated into the path. By the practice of shamatha-vipashyana, seeming obstacles can be accommodated on the spot through the sudden spark of awareness. The idea is not to react right away to either painful or pleasurable situations. Instead, once more, you should reflect on the exchange of sending and taking, or tonglen discipline. If you inherit a million dollars, you give it away, saying, 'This is not for me. It belongs to all sentient beings." If you are being sued for a million dollars, you say, "I will take the blame, and whatever positive comes out of this belongs to all sentient beings."

Obviously, there might be a problem when you first hear the good news or the bad news. At that point you go, "Aaah!" [Vidyadhara gasps.] That *aaah!* is some sort of ultimate bodhichitta. But after that, you need to cultivate relative bodhichitta, in order to make the whole thing pragmatic. Therefore, you practice the sending and taking of whatever is necessary. The important point is that when you take, you take the worst; and when you give, you give the best. So don't take any credit—unless you have been blamed. "I have been blamed for stealing all the shoes, and I take the credit!"

In some sense, when you begin to settle down to that kind of practice, to that level of being decent and good, you begin to feel very comfortable and relaxed in your world. It actually takes away your anxiety altogether, because you don't have to pretend at all. You have a general sense that you don't have to be defensive and you don't have to powerfully attack others anymore. There is so much accommodation taking place in you. And out of that comes a kind of power: what you say begins to make sense to others. The whole thing works so wonderfully. It does not have to become martyrdom. It works very beautifully.

That is the end of our discussion of the discipline of carrying whatever occurs in our life onto the path, which is connected with patience and nonaggression.

..

POINT FOUR

Showing the Utilization of Practice in One's Whole Life

POINT FOUR AND THE PARAMITA
OF EXERTION

The fourth point of the seven points of mind training is connected with the paramita of exertion. Exertion basically means being free from laziness. When we use the word *lazy*, we are talking about a general lack of mindfulness and a lack of joy in discipline. When your mind is mixed with dharma, when you have already become a dharmic person, then the connection has already been made. Therefore, you have no problem dealing with laziness. But if you have not made that connection, there might be some problems.

We could discuss exertion in terms of developing joy and appreciation for what you are doing. It is like taking a holiday trip: you are very inspired to wake up in the morning because you are expecting to have a tremendous experience. Exertion is like the minute before you wake up on a holiday trip: you have some sense of trusting that you are going to have a good time, but at the same time you have to put your effort into it. So exertion is some kind of celebration and joy, which is free from laziness.

It has been said in the scriptures that without exertion you cannot journey on the path at all. We have also said that without the legs of discipline you cannot walk on the path—but even if you have those legs, if you don't have exertion, you can't take any steps. Exertion involves a sense of pushing yourself step by step, little by little. You are actually connecting yourself to the path as you are walking on it. Nevertheless, you are also experiencing some sense of resistance. But that resistance could be overcome by overcoming laziness, by ceasing to dwell in the entertainment of your subconscious gossip, discursive thoughts, and emotionalism of all kinds.

The fourth point of mind training deals with completing your training in your life altogether, from the living situation you are in now until your death. So we are discussing what you can do while you are alive and when you are dying. These two slogans are instructions on how to lead your life.

17

Practice the five strengths,
The condensed heart instructions.

We have five types of energizing factors, or five strengths, so that we can practice our bodhisattva discipline throughout our whole life: strong determination, familiarization, seed of virtue, reproach, and aspiration.

Strong Determination

Number one is strong determination. You are determined to maintain twofold bodhichitta. The practitioner should always have the attitude of maintaining bodhichitta—for this lifetime, this year, this month, this day. Strong determination means not wasting your time. It is also making it a point that you and the practice are one. Practice is your way of strengthening yourself. Sometimes when you get up in the morning, particularly if you have had a late night or you have been partying, you feel very feeble, somewhat uncertain. Quite possibly you wake up with a hangover, feeling very guilty. You wonder whether you were foolish the night before, whether you did absurd things. You wonder what other people think of you and begin to be afraid that they might have lost their respect for you or that they might have confirmed your feebleness. You do a lot of worrying in that kind of situation.

The idea of the first strength is that as soon as you open your eyes and look out the window, as soon as you wake up, you reaffirm your strong determination to continue with your bodhichitta practice. And you do the same thing when you lie down on your bed at the end of the day, as you reflect back on your day's work, its problems, its frustrations, its pleasures, and all the good and bad things that happened. As you are dozing off, you think with strong determination that as soon as you wake up in the morning you are going to maintain your practice with continual exertion, which means joy. So you have some sense of looking forward to tomorrow, an attitude of looking forward to your day when you wake up in the morning.

Strong determination is connected with developing an attitude toward your practice that is almost like falling completely in love. You would like to go to bed with your lover; you long for it. You would like to wake up with your lover; you long for that, too. You have a sense of appreciation and joy; therefore, your practice does not become torture or torment, it does not become a cage. Instead, your practice becomes a way of cheering yourself up constantly. Your practice might require a certain amount of exertion, a certain amount of pushing yourself, but you are well connected, so you are pleased to wake up in the morning and you are pleased to go to bed at night. Even your sleep becomes worthwhile; you sleep in a good frame of mind. The idea is one of waking up basic goodness, the alaya principle, and realizing that you are in the right spot, the right practice. So there is a sense of joy in strong determination, which is the first strength.

Familiarization

The second strength is known as familiarization. Because you have already developed strong determination, everything becomes a natural process. Even if you sometimes are mindless, even if you lose your concentration or your awareness, situations will remind you to go back to your practice. This is a process of familiarization in which your dharmic subconscious gossip has begun to become more powerful than your ordinary subconscious gossip. Bodhichitta has become familiar ground in whatever you do—whether vice, virtue, or in between. So you are getting used to bodhichitta as an ongoing realization.

Again, this process is analogous to falling in love. When somebody mentions your lover's name, you feel both pain and pleasure. You feel turned on to that person's name and to anything associated with him or her. In the same way, the natural tendency of mindfulness-awareness, when the concept of egolessness has already evolved in your mind, is to flash on to dharma. You familiarize yourself with it. In other words, you no longer regard dharma as a foreign entity, but you begin to realize that dharma is a household thought, a household word, and a household activity. Each time you uncork your bottle of wine or unpop your Coca-Cola can or pour yourself a glass of water—whatever you do becomes a reminder. You cannot get rid of it; it becomes a natural situation.

So you learn to live with your sanity. That is very hard for many people at the beginning, but once you begin to realize that sanity is part of your being, there shouldn't be any problem. Of course, occasionally you want to take a break. You want to run away and take a vacation from your sanity. You want to do something else. However, your basic strength begins to become more powerful, so that your basic wickedness or insanity is changed into mindfulness and realization and familiarity with wakefulness.

Seed of Virtue

Number three is known as the seed of virtue. You have tremendous yearning all the time, so you do not take a rest from your wakefulness. It means not taking a break from your practice, basically speaking, but continuing on—not being content with what you are doing and not taking a break. You do not feel that you have had enough of it or that you have to do something else instead.

At that point, your neurosis about individual freedom and human rights might come up. You might begin to think, "I have a right to do anything I want, and I want to dive to the bottom of hell. I love it! I like it!" That kind of reactionism could happen. But you should pull yourself back up from the bottom of hell—for your own sake. You should realize that you cannot just give in to the little claustrophobia of your own sanity. In this case, virtue means that your body, speech, and mind are all dedicated to propagating bodhichitta in yourself.

Reproach

Number four is reproach, reproaching your ego. It is revulsion with samsara. Whenever any ego-centered thought occurs, you should think, "It is because of such clinging to ego that I wander in samsara and suffer endless pain. Since ego-clinging is the source of pain, if I try to maintain ego, there can be no happiness. Therefore, I must try to tame ego as much as I can." If you even want to talk to yourself, you should talk in this way. In fact, sometimes talking to yourself is very highly recommended, but it obviously depends on what you talk to yourself about. In this case, you are encouraged to say to your ego: "You have created tremendous trouble for me, and I don't like you. You have caused me so much trouble by making me wander in the lower realms of samsara. I have no desire at all to hang around with you. I'm going to destroy you. This 'you'—who are you, anyway? Go away! I don't like you."

Talking to your ego, reproaching yourself in that way, is very helpful. It is worth taking a shower and talking to yourself that way. It is worth sitting on the toilet seat and talking to yourself in that way. It would be a very good thing for you to do when you are driving. Instead of turning on the punk-rock, just turn on your reproach to your ego instead and talk to yourself. If you are being accompanied by somebody you might feel embarrassed, but you can still whisper to yourself. That is the best way to become an eccentric bodhisattva.

Aspiration

Number five is aspiration. The practitioner should end each session of meditation practice with the wish (1) to save all sentient beings—by himself, single-handedly; (2) not to forget twofold bodhichitta, even in his or her dreams; and (3) to apply bodhichitta in spite of whatever chaos and obstacles may arise. Because you have experienced joy and celebration in your practice, it does not feel like a burden to you. Therefore, you aspire further and further. You would like to attain enlightenment. You would like to free yourself from neurosis. You would also like to serve all "mother sentient beings"[1] throughout all times, all situations, at any moment. You are willing to become a rock or a bridge or a highway. You are willing to serve any worthy cause that will help the rest of the world. This is the same basic kind of aspiration as in taking the bodhisattva vow. It is also general instruction on becoming a very pliable person, so that the rest of the world can use you as a working basis for their enjoyment of sanity.

18

The mahayana instruction for ejection of consciousness at death Is the five strengths: how you conduct yourself is important.

The second slogan of the fourth point of mind training is dealing with the future—our death. The question of death is very important. Realizing the truth of suffering and impermanence is a very important first step in realizing the Buddha's teaching altogether. All of us will die sooner or later. Some of us will die very soon and some of us might die somewhat later, but that is not particularly a reason for relaxing.

I would like to discuss the idea of making friends with our death. According to the tradition of ego-oriented culture, death is seen as a defeat and as an insult. Theistic disciplines try to teach us to develop a sense of eternity. But the basic Buddhist tradition, particularly the mahayana, teaches us that death is a deliberate act. Because we have been born, we have to die. That is a very obvious and sensible thing to say. But beyond that, we can make friends with our death and see how we can die as we are.

People usually try to ignore their death completely. If you say to somebody, "Do you realize that you could die tomorrow?" that person will say, "Don't be silly! I'm okay." That attitude is an attempt to avoid the fundamental ugliness existing in us. But death need not be regarded as the ultimate ugly situation that happens to us; instead it can be regarded as a way of extending ourselves into the next life. In this case, death is seen as an invitation to allow this thing we cherish so very much, called our body, to perish. We shave and we take showers and baths and we clothe ourselves quite beautifully, or somewhat beautifully. On the whole, we try to take very good care of this pet called our body. It is like having a little puppy—we don't want our pet to die. But this little pet called our body might leave us sooner or later—*will* leave us sooner or later.

So to begin with, we have to realize that anything could happen to any one of us. We could be very healthy—but we might not die from ill health, we could die from an accident. We could die from sickness, from terminal diseases of all kinds, and sometimes we die without any reason at all. Although we have no external or internal problems—we just suddenly perish. We run completely out of breath and drop dead on the spot. So the point is to familiarize ourselves completely with our own death.

You want to live so much, and in order to live you can't do this and you can't do that. You cannot even sit on a zafu [meditation cushion] properly because your fear of death is so strong that you think the circulation in your legs might be cut off. You are so afraid to die that any attack that comes to you, even a little splinter in your finger, means death. So this instruction on how to die is not necessarily only about how to die when your death comes to you, but it is also a question of having to realize that death is always there.

One of the Kadam teachers who did these practices always put his drinking cup upside down on his table when he went to bed. Traditionally that means you are not going to be at home. You put your cup upside down so it won't get dusty. In that way you keep it clean and pure, so that somebody else can use it. The point is that the teacher always thought he might die that night; therefore he turned his cup upside down. You might think that is rather an eccentric way of going about things, but still, you should think twice or thrice when you say good night to somebody. You don't know whether or not you are going to see him or her tomorrow. That is a somewhat grim approach, if you view death as a disaster. But if you say good night nicely to somebody, that is a nice way to get out of your life, your body. It is a very humorous way of ending your life. There is a glory and humor in it. You don't need to die filled with remorse; you could die happily.

Like the last, this slogan is connected with the paramita of exertion. Exertion is a sense of joy in your practice. If you have practiced as much as you can in this life and are about to die, then if somebody says, "Look here, it is going to be very difficult for you to go beyond; may I pull the plug for you?," you should have learned to be able to say, "Yes, of course," and "Have a nice time." Plug pulled out.

After all, death is not that grim. It's just that we are actually embarrassed talking about it. Nowadays people have no problem talking about sex, or going to porno movies, but they have difficulty dealing with death. We are so embarrassed. It is a big deal to us, yet we have never actually wanted to reflect on death. We disregard the whole thing. We prefer to celebrate life rather than to prepare for death, or even to celebrate death.

In Shambhala terms, refusing to relate with death is connected with what is called setting-sun logic. The whole philosophy of setting sun is to prevent the message of death altogether. It is about how to beautify ourselves, our bodies, so that we could become living corpses. The idea of a living corpse is contradictory in some sense, but it makes sense in terms of setting-sun vision: if we don't want to die, our corpse has to live a long time; it has to become a living corpse.

Unlike that logic, or the many points of view like that, this slogan tells us that it is important for us to realize that death is an important part of our practice, since we are all going to die and since we are all going to relate with our death anyway. It is about how to die from the basic point of view of our own practice.

The instruction for how to die in mahayana is the five strengths. So we have the five strengths, or the five powers, once again. Because these practices are very simple, and because this is the same list we just discussed, we don't have to go into them in great detail. Applying the five strengths in this connection is very simple and straightforward.

Strong determination, number one, is connected with taking a very strong stand: "I will maintain my basic egolessness, my basic sanity, even in my death." You should concentrate on twofold bodhichitta, repeating to yourself: "Before death and during the *bardo*, in all my births may I not be separated from twofold bodhichitta."

Familiarization is developing a general sense of mindfulness and awareness so that you do not panic because you are dying. You should develop the strength of familiarization, reminding yourself repeatedly of twofold bodhichitta.

The *seed of virtue* is connected with not resting, not taking any kind of break from your fear of death. It also has to do with overcoming your attachment to your belongings.

Reproach means realizing that this so-called ego does not actually exist. Therefore, you can say, "What am I afraid of, anyway? Go away, ego." Recognizing that all problems come from ego, all death is caused by ego, you develop revulsion for ego and vow to overcome it.

And the last one, *aspiration*, is realizing that you have tremendous strength and desire to continue and to open yourself up. Therefore, you have nothing to regret when you die. You have already accomplished everything that you can accomplish. You have done everything: you have become a good practitioner and developed your basic practice completely; you have realized the meaning of shamatha and vipashyana, and you have realized the meaning of bodhichitta. If possible you should practice the sevenfold service, or *puja*.[2] But if you cannot do that, you should think: "Through all my lives may I practice the precious bodhichitta. May I meet a guru who will teach me that. Please, three jewels, bless me so that I may do that."

Beyond all that, there is an interesting twist. The ultimate instruction on death is simply to try to rest your mind in the nature of ultimate bodhichitta. That is to say, you rest your mind in the nature of alaya and try to pass your breath in that way until you are actually dead.

∴

POINT FIVE

Evaluation of Mind Training

POINT FIVE AND THE PARAMITA
OF MEDITATION

The fifth category of mind training is connected with the paramita of meditation. The idea of the paramita of meditation is basically that you are beginning to catch some possibility of the fever of knowledge, or prajna, already. Therefore, you begin to develop a tremendous sense of awareness and mindfulness. It has been said that the practice of meditation, that kind of mindfulness and awareness, is like protecting yourself from the lethal fangs of wild animals. These wild animals are related to the *kleshas*, the neurosis we experience. If there is not the mindfulness and awareness practice of the paramita of meditation, then we have no way of protecting ourselves from those attacks, and we also have no facilities to teach others or to work for the liberation of other sentient beings. That particular concept of meditation permeates this next section of lojong.

19

All dharma agrees at one point.

In this case, *dharma* has nothing to do with the philosophical term *dharma*, or "things as they are"; *dharma* here simply means "teachings." We could say that all teachings are basically a way of subjugating or shedding our ego. And depending on how much the lesson of the subjugation of ego is taking hold in us, that much reality is presented to us. All dharmas that have been taught are connected with that. There is no other dharma. No other teachings exist, particularly in the teachings of Buddha.

In this particular journey the practitioner can be put on a scale, and his or her commitment can be measured. It is like the scale of justice: if your ego is very heavy, you go down; if your ego is light, you go up. So giving up our personal project of ego-aggrandizement and attaining the impersonal project of enlightenment depends on how heavy-handed or how open you are.

Whether teachings are hinayana or mahayana, they all agree. The purpose of all of them is simply to overcome ego. Otherwise, there is no purpose at all. Whatever sutras, scriptures, or commentaries on the teachings of Buddhism you read, they should all connect with your being and be understood as ways of taming your ego. This is one of the main differences between theism and nontheism. Theistic traditions tend to build up an individual substance of some kind, so that you can then step out and do your own version of so-called bodhisattvic actions. But in the nontheistic Buddhist tradition, we talk in terms of having no being, no characteristics of egohood, and therefore being able to perform a much broader version of bodhisattva activity altogether.

The hinayana version of taming ego is to cut through sloppiness and wandering mind by the application of shamatha discipline, or mindfulness. Shamatha practice cuts through the fundamental mechanism of ego, which is that ego has to maintain itself by providing lots of subconscious gossip and discursive thoughts. Beyond that, the vipashyana principle of awareness also allows us to cut through our ego. Being aware of the whole environment and bringing that into our basic discipline allows us to become less self-centered and more in contact with the world around us, so there is less reference point to "me" and "my"-ness.

In the mahayana, when we begin to realize the bodhisattva principle through practicing bodhichitta, our concern is more with warmth and skillfulness. We realize we have nothing to hang on to in ourselves, so we can give away each time. The basis of such compassion is nonterritoriality, non-ego, no ego *at all*. If you have that, then you have compassion. Then further warmth and workability and gentleness take place as well. "All dharma agrees at one point" means that if there is no ego-clinging, then all dharmas are one, all teachings are one. That is compassion.

In order to have an affectionate attitude to somebody else, you have to be without ground to begin with. Otherwise you become an egomaniac, trying to attract people out of your seduction and passion alone, or your arrogance. Compassion develops from shunyata, or nonground, because you have nothing to hold on to, nothing to work *with*, no project, no personal gain, no ulterior motives. Therefore, whatever you do is a clean job, so to speak. So compassion and shunyata work together. It is like sunning yourself at the beach: for one thing you have a beautiful view of the sea and ocean and sky and everything, and there is also sunlight and heat and the ocean coming toward you.

In the hinayana, our ego begins to get a haircut; its beard is shaved. In the mahayana, the limbs of ego are cut, so there are no longer any arms and legs. We even begin to open up the torso of ego. By developing ultimate bodhichitta, we take away the heart so that nothing exists at all. Then we try to utilize the leftover mess of cut-off arms and legs and heads and hearts, along with lots of blood. Applying the bodhisattva approach, we make use of them, we don't throw them away. We don't want to pollute our world with lots of leftover egos. Instead we bring them onto the path of dharma by examining them and making use of them. So whatever happens in your life becomes a way of measuring your progress on the path—how much you have been able to shed your limbs, your torso, and your heart. That is why this slogan goes along with another saying of the Kadampa teachers, which is, "The shedding of ego is the scale that measures the practitioner." If you have more ego, you will be heavier on that scale; if you have less ego, you will be lighter. That is the measure of how much meditation and awareness have developed, and how much mindlessness has been overcome.

20

Of the two witnesses, hold the principal one.

In any situation there are two witnesses: other people's view of you and your own view of yourself. Of those, the principal witness is your own insight. You should not just go along with other people's opinion of you. The practice of this slogan is always to be true to yourself. Usually when you do something, you would like to get some kind of feedback from your world. You have your own opinions of how well you have done, and you also have other people's opinions of how well you have done. Usually you keep your own opinion of yourself to yourself. First you have your own opinions about something, and then you begin to branch out and ask somebody else: "Was that all right? How do you think I'm doing?" That is one of the traditional questions that comes up in meetings between teacher and student.

In many cases, people are very impressed by you because you look fit and you are cheerful a great deal and you seem to know what you are doing. A lot of compliments take place. On the other hand, a lot of criticism could come to you from others who do not properly and fully know what is actually happening within you. This slogan says that of the two witnesses, hold the principal one as the actual, authentic one. That authentic witness is you.

You are the only person who knows yourself. You are the only person who has been with yourself since you were born. And even before that, you carried your own great baggage of karma with you. You decided to enter the womb of somebody or other; you were born in somebody's stomach and you came out of it and you still carry your baggage along with you. You feel your own pain and pleasure and everything. You are the one who experienced your infancy, the pain and pleasure of it; you have gone through your teenagehood, the pain and pleasure of it; you are the one experiencing your adulthood, the pain and pleasure of it. You are beginning to experience your middle-age years, the pain and pleasure of it; and finally, you will experience getting old and dying, the pain and pleasure of it. You have never been away from yourself for even a minute. You know yourself so well. Therefore, you are the best judge of yourself. You know how naughty you are, you know how you try to be sensible, and you know how you sometimes try to sneak things in.

Usually "I" is talking to "am." "Am I to do this? Am I to do something naughty? If I do, nobody will know." Only *we* know. We could do it and we might get away with it. There are lots of tricks or projects you and yourself always do together, hoping that nobody will actually find out. If you had to lay the whole thing out in the open, it would be so embarrassing. You would feel so strange. On the other hand, of course, there is the other possibility. You could try to be very good so that somebody would be so impressed with you and with how much effort you put into yourself. You might try to be a good boy or a good girl. But if you have to spell the whole thing out, nobody will actually believe how good you are trying to be. People would think it was just a joke.

Only you really know yourself. You know at every moment. You know the way you do things: the way you brush your teeth, the way you comb your hair, the way you take your shower, the way you put on your clothes, the way you talk to somebody else, the way you eat, even if you are not terribly hungry. During all of those things, "I" and "am" are still carrying on a conversation about everything else. So there are a lot of unsaid things happening to you all the time. Therefore, the principal witness, or the principal judge, is yourself. The judgment of how you are progressing in your lojong practice is yours.

You know best about yourself, so you should work with yourself constantly. This is based on trusting your intelligence rather than trusting yourself, which could be very selfish. It is trusting your intelligence by knowing who you are and what you are. You know yourself so well, therefore any deception could be cut through. If someone congratulates or compliments you, they may not know your entire existence. So you should come back to your own judgment, to your own sense of your expressions and the tricks you play on others and on yourself. That is not self-centered, it is self-inspired from the point of view of the nonexistence of ego. You just witness what you are. You are simply witnessing and evaluating the merit, rather than going back over it in a Jungian or Freudian way.

21

Always maintain only a joyful mind.

The point of this slogan is continuously to maintain joyful satisfaction. That means that every mishap is good, because it is encouragement for you to practice the dharma. Other people's mishaps are good also: you should share them and bring them into yourself as the continuity of their practice or discipline. So you should include that also. It is very nice to feel that way, actually.

For myself, there is a sense of actual joy. You feel so good and so high. I suppose I was converted into Buddhism. Although I was not sticking bumper stickers on my car saying, "Jesus saved me," I was doing that mentally. Mentally I was putting on bumper stickers saying, "I'm glad that my ego has been converted into Buddhism and that I've been accepted and realized as a Buddhist citizen, a compassionate person." I used to feel extraordinarily good and so rewarded. Where that came from was no question: I felt so strong and strengthened by the whole thing. In fact, I began to feel that if I didn't have that kind of encouragement in myself, I would have a lot of difficulty studying the vajrayana. I felt so grateful, so good. So this slogan means to maintain a sense of satisfaction and joyfulness in spite of all the little problems and hassles in one's life.

This slogan is connected to the previous one. ["Of the two witnesses, hold the principal one."] If you have been raised in the Judeo-Christian tradition of discipline, the idea of watching yourself is based purely on guilt. But in this case, it is not that way. We do not have any logic that acknowledges, understands, or presents a concept like original sin. From our point of view, you are not basically condemned. Your naughtiness is not necessarily regarded as your problem—although it *is* witnessed, obviously. You are not fundamentally condemned; your temporary naughtinesses are regarded as coming from temporary problems only. Therefore, to follow up on that, this slogan says, "Always maintain only a joyful mind." It is a joyful mind because you do not have to be startled by any situation of wretchedness or, for that matter, sudden upliftedness. Instead, you can maintain a sense of cheerfulness all along.

To start with, you maintain a sense of cheerfulness because you are on the path; you are actually doing something about yourself. While most sentient beings have no idea what should be done with themselves, at least you have some lead on it, which is fantastic. If you step out into Brooklyn or the Black Hole of Calcutta, you will realize that what we are trying to do with ourselves is incredible. Generally, nobody has the first idea about anything like this at all. It is incredible, fantastic. You should be tremendously excited and feel wonderful that somebody even thought of such an idea.

There is a sense of joy from that point of view, a sense of celebration which you can refer to whenever you feel depressed, whenever you feel that you do not have enough in the environment to cheer you up, or whenever you feel that you do not have the kind of feedback you need in order to practice. The idea is that whether it is a rainy day, a stormy day, a sunny day, a very hot day, or a very cold day, whether you are hungry, thirsty, very full, or very sick—you can maintain a sense of cheerfulness. I do not think I have to explain that too much. There is a sense of basic cheerfulness that allows you to wake yourself up.

That joy seems to be the beginning of compassion. We could say that this slogan is based on how to go about maintaining your awareness of the practice of mahayana—literally and fully. You might feel uptight about somebody's terrible job, that his or her particular shittiness has been transferred onto you and has fucked up the whole environment. But in this case, you don't blame such a person, you blame yourself. And blaming yourself is a delightful thing to do. You begin to take a very cheerful attitude toward the whole thing. So you are transcending *oy vey*—getting out of Brooklyn, metaphorically speaking. You could do that. It is possible to do that.

This kind of cheerfulness has a lot of guts. It is founded in buddha nature, tathagatagarbha. It is founded in the basic compassion of people who have already done such a thing themselves: people like Avalokiteshvara, Manjushri, Jamgön Kongtrül, Milarepa, Marpa, and all the rest. So we could do it, too. It is founded on a real situation.

If someone punches you in the mouth and says, "You are terrible," you should be grateful that such a person has actually acknowledged you and said so. You could, in fact, respond with tremendous dignity by saying, "Thank you, I appreciate your concern." In that way his neurosis is taken over by you, taken into you, much as is done in tonglen practice. There is an immense sacrifice taking place here. If you think this is ridiculously trippy, you are right. In some sense the whole thing *is* ridiculously trippy. But if somebody doesn't begin to provide some kind of harmony, we will not be able to develop sanity in this world at all. Somebody has to plant the seed so that sanity can happen on this earth.

22

If you can practice even when distracted, you are well trained.

We have all kinds of situations that we have to handle in ordinary life, even states that we are not aware of, but we are not particularly concerned about our existence; we are more concerned with our neurosis and our games. If we are in a very high level of uptightness, as soon as that happens there is no awareness. But we can also immediately experience a sense of awareness. Traditionally, any chaos that came up was regarded as a shout for some kind of holiness or help, blessing or prayer. In our ordinary, everyday life, in theistic traditions also, each time something suddenly comes up, we say, "Goodness, look at that," or we utter sacred names. Traditionally that was supposed to be a reminder for awareness. But we never use it that way these days, we just use swear words in the most degrading way.

The idea of this slogan is the realization that whenever situations of an ordinary nature or extraordinary nature come up—our pot boils over, or our steak is turned into charcoal, or suddenly we slip and lose our grasp—a sudden memory of awareness should take place. Jamgön Kongtrül's commentary talks about a well-trained, powerful horse who loses his balance and suddenly regains it again through losing it. And the sutras talk about the bodhisattva's actions being like those of a well-trained athlete who slips on a slippery surface and in the process of slipping regains his or her balance by using the force of the slipping process. It is similar, I suppose, to skiing, where you use the force that goes down and let yourself slide down through the snow—suddenly you gain attention and develop balance out of that.

So whenever there is the sudden glimpse or sudden surprise of losing one's grip—that seeming fear of losing grip of one's reality can be included properly. To do so there is a need for renunciation. It is not your chauvinistic trip, that you are a fantastically powerful and strong person and also have a sense of mindfulness taking place all the time. But when something hits you, which is a result of unmindfulness, then suddenly that unmindfulness creates a reminder automatically. So you actually get back on track, so to speak, able to handle your life.

We begin to realize that we can actually practice in spite of our wandering thoughts. I'm sorry to be such a chauvinist, but let me give an example of that. What used to happen was that I would be terribly hurt, psychologically depressed, and pushed into dark corners by my good tutor and by my administration in Surmang monastery. When I was more remorseful, more sad, and more helpless—but carefully helpless, deliberately helpless—I used to think of my root teacher Jamgön Kongtrül and weep. After he departed from Surmang monastery, I kept thinking of him, and he actually did something to me, cheered me up. I used to try the vajrayana approach to devotion: I would say to all my attendants, "Go out! I don't need to observe teatime at this point; I'm going to read." Then I would lie back and cry for thirty minutes, or sometimes forty-five minutes. Then somebody would jump up. My attendants became very worried, thinking that I was sick or something. And I would say: "Send them back. Go away. I don't need any more tea."

But sometimes I found that was not very effective, that it was too early to introduce vajrayana devotion, because we didn't have enough basic training. So I developed a new tactic, which was purely in accordance with this slogan. Whenever there was any problem or chaos, I would tell Jamgön Kongtrül about it when I visited him, and when I came back, I began to use a new method. Whenever there was any chaos or problem, or even when there was goodness or a celebration—whenever *anything* happened—I would just come back to my existence and my memory of him, as well as my memory of the path and the practice. I began to be able to feel a sense of awareness, quick awareness, very direct awareness. This awareness was not necessarily related with the memory of Jamgön Kongtrül; it was the awareness that comes when you are just drifting off and the process of drifting off brings you back. That is what is meant here. For instance, if you are a good rider, your mind might be wandering, but you will not fall off your horse. In other words, even if you are drifting off, if that process of drifting off can bring you back, that is the mark of perfect practice.

The idea is that you have been trained already, so you will not have any problem in continuing. When pleasurable or painful circumstances hit, you do not become their slave. You have learned how to reflect suddenly on tonglen and on bodhichitta mind, so you are not subject to extreme pleasure and extreme pain or depression at all. When you meet with a situation, that situation affects your emotions and your state of mind. But whenever your state of mind and your emotions are affected, because of that jolt, suddenly the situation itself becomes your awareness and your mindfulness. It comes to you, so there is less need for you to put effort into it from your end. You do not have to try to protect, to understand, or to be watchful. That does not mean that you should just give up and things will come to you all the time. There is obviously a need for you to develop basic awareness and mindfulness and to be alert altogether. But that alertness could be a fundamental frame of mind, which is connected with the paramita of meditation.

What we have been discussing in point five is quite straightforward. The main point is not to let yourself be wounded by the fangs of neurosis, the fangs of the kleshas. The way to do that is to realize that "all dharma agrees at one point," which is the taming of one's ego. That is the scale on which practitioners can be weighed. "Of the two witnesses, hold the principal one" means to start with your own judgment of how you are doing. "Always maintain only a joyful mind" means having a sense of cheerfulness. Because you are not trapped in heavy-handed discipline, you can experience a sense of joy, particularly when extremely evil or extremely joyful situations occur to you. And the mark of being well trained is that you can practice even when distracted.

If you practice some of this, I am sure we will not have any problem in producing thousands of buddhas and bodhisattvas in this century!

POINT SIX

Disciplines of Mind Training

POINT SIX AND PRAJNAPARAMITA

The paramita associated with the sixth point of mind training is prajnaparamita. These slogans are all connected with sharpening your intelligence in order to work with yourself. That is the idea of the sword of prajna. Prajna is regarded as the sword that cuts the bondage of ego. The way to cut the bondage of ego in mahayana practice is basically the same as in vipashyana practice—it is awareness, relating to the rest of your world and to your life. It is connected with a larger sense of your entire life and particularly with postmeditation experience.

Whatever occurs in your life is governed by prajna, which cuts through habitual or potential neurosis. Applying that tremendous sense of mindfulness and awareness comes from the great concentration that is developed through the bodhisattva path. With the help of the shamatha and vipashyana principles, you learn how to consolidate yourself as a mahayana practitioner—being in a state of compassion, kindness, openness, and gentleness.

On the other hand, you are also in a state of egolessness. There is no clinging, no working or dwelling on anything connected with ego, *atman* or soul. When you are not dwelling on anything connected with ego, the activities described in the lojong text begin to permeate your life. They begin to manifest. You realize that there is no "I" to meditate on and, for that matter, no "I am" to propagate your existence. Because of that, you are able to exchange yourself for others. By first becoming able to sacrifice yourself, you are able to overcome obstacles. Then you can relate with the rest of the world. In that way, you learn how to deal with your journey on the path by means of the sword of prajna.

23
Always abide by the three basic principles.

This slogan is a general description as to how we can practice the buddhadharma according to the three basic principles of hinayana, mahayana, and vajrayana. It is connected with a sense of keeping the discipline of all three yanas—hinayana mindfulness practice, mahayana benevolence, and vajrayana crazy wisdom—all at the same time.

We may begin to behave in a crazy style unfounded in any particular tradition and disregard the dignity of other traditions, disrupting whole social setups founded on such religious traditions. That is not supposed to happen. We can actually relieve ourselves from doing such frivolous things. Basing our spiritual practice on our own self-snugness and self-delight seems to be one of the most dangerous things of all. We have our trip together: our philosophy is worked out, our quotations are on time; we have our grammar and language already set up—but after all that, we don't want to give up our ego. We have some kind of ground to walk on, and we do not want to give up our most sacred and secret property. That becomes problematic; we are not actually following the journey properly. The text says that dharma should not be perverted on the basis of happiness, which in this case is any kind of confirmation existing within the dharmic realm.

The three basic principles are also described as [1] keeping the two vows, [2] refraining from outrageous action, and [3] developing patience.

The first is keeping the promises you made when you took the refuge and bodhisattva vows, keeping them completely. This one is quite straightforward.

Number two is refraining from outrageous action. When you begin to practice lojong, you realize that you shouldn't have any consideration for yourself; therefore, you try to act in a self-sacrificing manner.

But often your attempt to manifest selflessness becomes exhibitionism. You let yourself be thrown in jail or crucified on a cross. You manifest unselfish actions because of your convictions—your so-called convictions in this case—but your actions are still based on your *idea* of being a decent person. You might act on a whim or become very crazy, involving yourself in unselfish exhibitionism of all kinds, such as going on long fasts or lying down in the street in the name of bodhisattva practice. Many of our American friends have done just those things. However, that approach should be regarded as pure exhibitionism rather than as the accomplishment of bodhisattva action.

Number three is developing patience. Usually, there is extreme confusion about patience. That is to say, you can be patient with your friends but you cannot be patient with your enemies; you can be patient with people whom you are trying to cultivate or your particular protégés, but you cannot be patient with those who are outside of your protégé-ism. That kind of extreme is actually a form of personality cult, the cult of yourself, which is not such a good idea. In fact, it has been said that it is absolutely *not* a good idea.

Through prajna you realize how much you are trying to become something. Having become somewhat accomplished in lojong practice and in tonglen training, you may begin to feel that it is time for you to branch out and become a leader or a hero. But you should watch out for that. This is one of the basic points of conduct discipline. It is connected with the paramita of prajna: because you begin to discriminate who you are, what you are, and what you are doing, you are constantly watchful of all of that.

24

Change your attitude, but remain natural.

Generally, our attitude is that we always want to protect our own territory first. We want to preserve our own ground—others come afterward. The point of this slogan is to change that attitude around, so that we actually reflect on others first and on ourselves later. It is very simple and direct. You usually practice gentleness and tenderness toward yourself, and the opposite of that toward others. If you want something from outside, you will send someone else to get it for you instead of going out and getting it yourself. So this slogan applies to the attempt to impose your power and your authority on others. You also try to get away with things. For instance, you don't wash the dishes, hoping that somebody else will do it. Changing your attitude means reversing your attitude altogether—instead of making someone else do something, you do it yourself.

Then the slogan says "remain natural," which has a sense of relaxation. It means taming your basic being, taming your mind altogether so that you are not constantly pushing other people around. Instead, you take the opportunity to blame yourself.

We are talking about changing your attitude of cherishing yourself. Instead of cherishing yourself, you cherish others—and then you just relax. That's it. It's very simple-minded.

25

Don't talk about injured limbs.

Because of your arrogance and your aggression, you prefer to talk about other people's defects as a way of building yourself up. The point of this slogan is *not* taking delight in somebody else's defects or injured limbs. "Injured limbs" refers very literally to people's psychological or physical state: being blind or dumb or slow. It refers to all kinds of physical defects that a person might possess. This seems to be the general ethic already set up by Christianity, that nobody should be condemned on account of his or her physical defects, but everybody is regarded as a person. We generally don't do that anyway, in any case.

This is not a puritanical approach to reality, but simply realizing that if a person has problems in dealing with his or her life, we do not have to exaggerate that by making remarks about it. We could simply go along with that person's problems. If somebody is completely freaked out and exaggerating his or her particular realm of phenomena, or freaked out about having an encounter with somebody, that is not regarded as an ugly manifestation of that person. It is just a general sense of his or her response to reality, which takes place all the time.

26

Don't ponder others.

In this slogan, "pondering others" means picking on other people's little misgivings and problems. One of the problems we have generally is that when somebody does something to us or violates our principles, we keep picking on that particular thing. We would like to get at him and make sure that person's problems are subject to attack, subject to unhealthiness. For instance, because you have labored through your tonglen practice and worked so hard, you develop tremendous arrogance. You feel as though you have gone through so much and that your effort makes you a worthy person. So when you meet somebody who has not accomplished what you have, you would like to put them down. This slogan is very simple: don't do that.

I do not think there is very much difference between this slogan and the preceding one; they are basically saying the same thing. Both slogans are very simple and direct. All the slogans are points which come to you—not particularly traffic signs but reminders. And each time a particular point occurs to you, the slogans as a whole become more meaningful.

27

Work with the greatest defilements first.

You should work with whatever is your greatest obstacle first—whether it is aggression, passion, pride, arrogance, jealousy, or what have you. You should not just say, "I will sit more first, and will deal with that later." Working with the greatest defilements means working with the highlights of your experience or your problems. You do not just want to work with chicken shit, you want to work with the chicken itself.

If we have philosophical, metaphysical, poetic, artistic, or technological hang-ups related with our particular neurosis, we should bring them out first rather than last. When we have a hang-up, we should work with that hang-up. It has been said that all dharmas should be applied in trying to tame it, but at the same time we should not try to arrive at certain results. So the idea is to purify and to work on the highlights that come up rather than regarding them as junk. We simply work on any highlight or problem that comes up in our state of mind directly and straightforwardly.

28

Abandon any hope of fruition.

This slogan means that you should give up possibilities of becoming the greatest person in the world by means of your training. In particular, you may quite impatiently expect that because of lojong practice you will become a better person. You may be hoping that you will be invited to more little clubs and gatherings by your protégés or friends, who are impressed with you. The point is that you have to give up any such possibility; otherwise, you could become an egomaniac. In other words, it is too early for you to collect disciples.

Working with the slogans does not mean looking for temporary revelation or trying to achieve something by doing little smart things that have managed to quell people's problems in the past. You may have become a great speaker by giving one talk or a great psychologist who has managed to conquer other people's neuroses or a great literary figure who has written several books or a famous musician who has produced several albums. Such things are somewhat based on relating with reality properly, being connected with reality. But you want to subjugate the world in your own particular style, however subtle and sneaky that may be.

By doing the same kind of trick, you hope to attain enlightenment. You have tuned in to a professional approach and become a professional achiever. So there is the possibility that you might approach practice in the same way, thinking that you can actually con the buddha mind within yourself and sneakily attain enlightenment. That seems to be the problem referred to in this particular slogan. It says in the commentary that any pursuit of this life's happiness, joy, fame, or wisdom, or the hope of attaining some state of glorious liberation in the life hereafter, could be regarded as a problem.

29

Abandon poisonous food.

If the practice of egolessness begins to become just another way of building up your ego—building your ego by giving up your ego—it is like eating poisonous food; it will not take effect. In fact, rather than providing an eternally awakened state of mind, it will provide you with death, because you are holding on to your ego. So if your reason for sitting or doing postmeditation practice or any other kind of practice is self-improvement, it is like eating poisonous food. "If I sit properly, with the greatest discipline and exertion, then I will become the best meditator of all"—that is a poisonous attitude.

This is a very powerful slogan for us. It means that whatever we do with our practice, if that practice is connected with our personal achievement, which is called "spiritual materialism," or the individual glory that we are in the right and others are wrong, and we would like to conquer their wrongness or evil because we are on the side of God and so forth—that kind of bullshit or cow dung is regarded as eating poisonous food. Such food may be presented to us beautifully and nicely, but when we begin to eat it, it stinks.

30

Don't be so predictable.

The literal translation of this slogan is "Don't be consistent," but it is more like "Don't be so kind and faithful, so guileless." That is to say, an ordinary person or man of the world would have some understanding about his relationship with his enemies and his friends and how much debt he owes people. It is all very predictable. Similarly, when somebody inflicts pain on you, you keep that for long-term storage, long-term discussion, long-term resentment. You would eventually like to strike back at him, not forgetting his insult in ten or even twenty years.

This slogan has an interesting twist. To begin with, we could use the analogy of the trustworthy friend. Some people are trustworthy people, traditional people, maybe you could say old-fashioned people. When you become friends with people like that, they always remember your friendship, and the trust between you lasts for a very long time. In the example of the trustworthy person, you *should* always remember your connection with him or her and his or her connection with you. But if somebody gives you a bad deal, or if you have a lot of conflict with somebody, you should not constantly hold a grudge against him. In this case, the point is that you should *not* always remember someone's bad dealings with you. This slogan is somewhat confusing, but the point is to give up altogether your long memory of antagonism.

Usually everything we do is predictable. When we have something good happen—for instance, when someone brings us a bottle of champagne—we are always trying to repay that kindness with something else, like inviting them for dinner or saying nice things. And how we relate when something bad happens is the same. We are usually predictable in how we do that as well. Slowly we built up society out of that.

When somebody is about to inflict pain on us, we usually wait until they actually strike us and are unkind to us. We wait for that person to begin to write bad articles about us. Then we have made an enemy out of somebody. That is not the proper approach. The proper approach is to make friends immediately rather than waiting for something to strike. Instead of waiting until a person commits a sin or acknowledges his aggression toward you, you communicate immediately and directly. So you are communicating directly rather than waiting for strategy. That is precisely what the commentary says, and that is what we are trying to practice at this point.

31

Don't malign others.

You would like to put people in the wrong saying disparaging things. However pleasantly coated with sugar and ice cream, underneath you are trying to put people down, trying to get revenge. Disparaging people is based on showing off your own virtue. You think that your virtues can only show because other people's are lessened, because they are less virtuous than you are. This applies to both education and practice. You might have better training in the dharma and say, "Somebody's attention span in his shamatha practice is shorter than mine; therefore, I am better" or "Somebody knows fewer terms than I do." Fundamentally, these are all ways of saying, "That other person is stupid, and I am better than he is." I think this slogan is very straightforward.

32

Don't wait in ambush.

The Tibetan version of this slogan literally says, "Don't ambush," that is, wait for somebody to fall down so that you can attack. You are waiting for that person to fall into the trap or problem you want or expect. You want them to have that misfortune, and you hope that misfortune will take place in a way which will allow you to attack.

If you are having a disagreement with somebody, you don't usually attack him or her right away because you don't want to be in a powerless position. Instead, you wait for him to fall apart, and then you attack him. Sometimes you pretend to be his adviser, and you attack him in that disguise, pointing out to him how wretched he is. You say, "I have been waiting to tell you this. Now that you are falling apart completely, I am going to take the opportunity to tell you that you are not so good. I am in much better shape than you are." That is a sort of opportunism, a bandit's approach. That bandit's approach is the meaning of waiting in ambush, which happens quite frequently.

33

Don't bring things to a painful point.

Don't blame your sense of dissatisfaction, pain, and misery on somebody else, and do not try to lay your power trips on others. Whatever power you have—domestic power, literary power, or political power—don't impose it on somebody else.

This slogan also means not to humiliate people. An important point of the bodhisattva idea altogether is to encourage people on their path. However, you could relate with people in such a way that you progress much faster on the path than they do. There are ways of slowing down other people's journeys so that you can stay ahead of them. But in this slogan, instead of doing that, you develop the other way around—you come along behind the others.

34

Don't transfer the ox's load to the cow.

It is very easy to say, "It's not my fault, it's all your fault, it's always your fault." It is very easy to say that, but it is questionable. One has to think about one's problems personally, honestly, and genuinely. If there were no *you* to initiate situations, there would not be any problems at all. But since you exist, therefore there are also problems. We do not want to transfer that load.

The ox is capable of carrying burdens; the cow is less capable of carrying burdens. So the point of this slogan is that you do not transfer your heavy load to someone who is weaker than you. Transferring the ox's load to the cow means not wanting to deal with anything on your own. You don't want to take on any responsibilities; you just pass them on to your secretary or your friends or anybody you can order about. In English we call this "passing the buck." Doing that is a bad idea, since we are supposed to be cutting down chaos and creating less traffic in the samsaric world altogether. We are supposed to be cutting down on administrative problems and trying to sort things out. We could invite other people to be our helpers, but we cannot pass the buck to them. So don't transfer the ox's load to the cow.

35

Don't try to be the fastest.

When practitioners begin to develop their understanding of the dharma and their appreciation of the dharma, they sometimes fall into a sort of racehorse approach. They become involved with who is the fastest: who can understand the highest meaning of mahamudra or the greatest meaning of tantra or the highest idea of ultimate bodhichitta, or who has understood any of the hidden teachings. Such practitioners are concerned with who can do their prostrations faster, who can sit better, who can eat better, who can do this and that better. They are always trying to race with other people. But if our practice is regarded purely as a race, we have a problem. The whole thing has become a game rather than actual practice, and there is no seed of benevolence and gentleness in the practitioner. So you should not use your practice as a way to get ahead of your fellow students. The point of this slogan is not to try to achieve fame, honor, or distinction through one's practice.

36

Don't act with a twist.

Acting with a twist means that since you think you are going to get the best in any case, you might as well volunteer for the worst. That is very sneaky. You could act with a twist in dealing with your teacher, your students, your life situation—everything. You could pretend to be a completely benevolent person who always takes the blame, realizing all along that you are going to get the best. It is quite straightforward, I think.

Acting with a twist is a form of spiritual materialism. It is always having the ulterior motive of working for your own benefit. For instance, in order to gain good results for yourself, you may temporarily take the blame for something. Or you may practice lojong very hard in order to get something out of it, or with the idea of protecting yourself from sickness. The practice of this slogan is to drop that attitude of looking for personal benefits from practice—either as an immediate or a long-term result.

37

Don't make gods into demons.

This slogan refers to our general tendency to dwell on pain and go through life with constant complaints. We should not make painful that which is inherently joyful.

At this point, you may have achieved a certain level of taming yourself. You may have developed the tonglen practice of exchanging yourself for others and feel that your achievement is real. But at the same time, you are so arrogant about the whole thing that your achievement begins to become an evil intention, because you think you can show off. In that way, dharma becomes adharma, or nondharma.

Although your achievement may be the right kind of achievement and you may actually have a very good experience—if you regard that as a way of proving yourself and building up your ego, it is not so good.

38

Don't seek others' pain as the limbs of your own happiness.

This slogan is quite straightforward: you hope that somebody else will suffer so that you can benefit from it. Here is a very simple analogy: if a member of the sangha dies, you might inherit his or her meditation cushion, or if you are a vajrayana practitioner, you might inherit his bell and *dorje*. We could expand on that logic in any number of situations, but I don't think it is necessary for us to do so.

We should not build our own happiness on the suffering of others. Although it may benefit us if someone experiences misfortune, we should not wish for that and dream about what we could get out of such a situation. Happiness that is built on pain is spurious and only leads to depression in the long run.

POINT SEVEN

Guidelines of Mind Training

POINT SEVEN AND POSTMEDITATION

The guidelines of mind training have to do with how to proceed further in our everyday life. This topic seems to be connected with a general realization of how we can conduct ourselves properly in our relationships and in the general postmeditation experience.

39
All activities should be done with one intention.

The one intention is to have a sense of gentleness toward others and a willingness to be helpful to others—always. That seems to be the essence of the bodhisattva vow. In whatever you do—sitting, walking, eating, drinking, even sleeping—you should always take the attitude of being of benefit to all sentient beings.

40

Correct all wrongs with one intention.

When you are in the midst of perverse circumstances such as intense sickness, a bad reputation, court cases, economic or domestic crisis, increase of kleshas, or resistance to practice, you should develop compassion for all sentient beings who also suffer like this, and you should aspire to take on their suffering yourself through the practice of lojong.

We need to correct, or to overcome, all the wrongs or bad circumstances that we experience. Instead of having a negative attitude toward practice and not wanting to practice any longer—whenever such perversions and problems occur, they should be overcome. In other words, if your practice becomes good when things are good for you but becomes nonexistent when the situation is bad, that is not the way. Instead, whether situations are good or bad, you continue your practice.

To correct all wrongs means to stamp on the kleshas. Whenever you don't want to practice—stamp on that, and then practice. Whenever any bad circumstance comes up that might put you off—stamp on it. In this slogan you are deliberately, immediately, and very abruptly suppressing the kleshas.

41

Two activities: one at the beginning, one at the end.

The point of this slogan is to begin and end each day with twofold bodhichitta. In the morning you should remember bodhichitta and take the attitude of not separating yourself from it, and at the end of the day, you should examine what you have done. If you have not separated yourself from twofold bodhichitta, you should be delighted and vow to take the same attitude again the next day. And if you were separated from bodhichitta, you should vow to reconnect with it the next day.

This slogan is a very simple one. It means that your life is sandwiched by your vow to put others before yourself and by your sense of commitment to twofold bodhichitta. When you get up in the morning, as soon as you wake up, to start off your day you promise yourself that you will work on twofold bodhichitta and develop a sense of gentleness toward yourself and others. You promise not to blame the world and other sentient beings and to take their pain on yourself. When you go to bed, you do the same thing. In that way both your sleep and the day that follows are influenced by that commitment. It is quite straightforward.

42

Whichever of the two occurs, be patient.

Whether a joyful or a painful situation occurs, whatever happens to you, your practice is not swayed by it, but you maintain continual patience and continual practice. Whether you are in the midst of extreme happiness or extreme suffering, you should be patient. You should regard extreme suffering as the result of previous karma. Therefore, there is no need to feel remorseful. Instead you should simply try to purify any evil deeds and obscurations. Extreme happiness is also the result of previous karma, so there is no reason to indulge in it. You should donate any riches to virtuous causes, and your sense of personal authenticity and power should be resolved into virtue.

Quite often, when things are disturbing or problematic for students, they lose their sense of perspective and try to find some kind of scapegoat within the dharma. For instance, in order to justify their own inability to practice, they come up with all sorts of ideas: the environment is not right, their brothers and sisters in the practice situation are not right, the organization of the dharmic environment is not right. All sorts of complaints begin to come up. In extreme cases, people begin to take refuge in nondharmic people again and go back to situations in which their existence might be acknowledged. The idea in this slogan is to develop and maintain discipline so that whether situations are good or bad, you still maintain patience in your practice. The point is to be patient, which means taking more time and being forbearing.

43

Observe these two, even at the risk of your life.

You should maintain the disciplines you have committed yourself to: in particular, [1] the refuge vow and [2] the bodhisattva vow. You should maintain the general livelihood of being a decent Buddhist and, beyond that, the special discipline of the practice of lojong, or mind training. This practice should become a very important part of your life.

For tantric practitioners, this slogan means that in this life and in any future lives, you should keep the three-yana discipline. This applies to dharmic principles in general and to the practice of lojong in particular. You should always keep that bond, or *samaya*, even at the risk of your life.

44

Train in the three difficulties.

The three difficulties have to do with how we relate to our own kleshas, or neuroses. The first difficulty is to realize the point at which you are tricked by your own emotions, or kleshas. You must look and understand that trick, which is very difficult. The second difficulty is to dispel or to exorcise our emotionalism. And the third difficulty is to cut the continuity of that emotionalism. In other words, in the beginning it is very hard to recognize your neuroses; then it is very difficult to overcome them; and thirdly, it is very difficult to cut through them. Those are the three difficulties.

When neurosis arises, you first have to recognize it as neurosis. Then you have to apply a technique or antidote to overcome it. Since neurosis basically comes from selfishness, from placing too much importance on yourself, the antidote is that you have to cut through your ego. Finally, you have to have the determination not to follow the neurosis or continue to be attracted to it. There is a sense of abruptly overcoming neurosis.

All together we have six categories. The difficulties are: first, it is difficult to recognize our kleshas; second, it is difficult to overcome them; third, it is difficult to cut through them. What you should do is:

first, recognize them; second, try to overcome them; third, take a vow never to re-create such things again.

It is very difficult to relate with the bodhisattva principle, or for that matter, any monumental concept. Therefore, the slogan says, "Train in the three difficulties." But if you are willing to practice lojong, your mind will be completely trained and indoctrinated into the bodhisattva's way of thinking. In fact, *lojong* literally means "indoctrination": *lo* means "intelligence," and *jong* means "cleaning up" or "training." The idea is to indoctrinate yourself so that you cannot get away from that monolithic principle called buddha nature, bodhichitta, tathagatagarbha.

45
Take on the three principal causes.

"Cause" refers to that which causes you to be a good dharmic person or bodhisattva. The first cause is having a good teacher. The second cause is applying your mind and basic demeanor to the dharma. The third cause is having food and housing so that it is possible for you to practice the dharma. You should try to maintain those three situations and take delight that you have such opportunities.

To take on the first principal cause is to realize the necessity of the teacher, who actually allows you to get into situations.

To take on the second principal cause is to realize that one's mind should be tamed. For instance, your mind might be into a business deal, or a teaching deal, or a book-writing deal, or into making a funny kind of monumental experience for yourself. You might have all kinds of ambitions about your life. This attitude was not all that prominent in the days when Jamgön Konetrül wrote his commentary on the slogans, but today we have a lot more choices. You might think you can hunt animals by becoming a great Buddhist or a great bodhisattva or be a great author, a great prostitute, or a great salesman. But that state of mind, that type of ambition, is not all that good. Instead, you have to come to the point at which your state of mind would say, "I would like to devote myself to the dharma completely and fully."

To take on the third principal cause is to realize that it is possible for you to practice the dharma because of having the right circumstances, because you have been taking an open attitude toward your life and have already worked out some kind of livelihood. Your food and clothes and shelter are taken care of, and economically you can afford to practice.

So you should take on and practice these three causes: [1] working with a teacher, [2] training your mind, [3] establishing an economic base for practice.

46

Pay heed that the three never wane.

The first thing you should not let wane is devotion to your spiritual friend [kalyanamitra]. Your mental attitude of admiration, dedication, and gratefulness toward the spiritual friend should not diminish. The second thing you should not let wane is a delightful attitude toward lojong, or the taming of your mind. Your appreciation for receiving such teachings as lojong or mind training should not diminish. And the third thing you should not let wane is your conduct—the hinayana and mahayana vows that you have taken. Your practice of the hinayana and mahayana disciplines should not diminish.

This slogan is straight and low-key. At this point, in practicing mahayana, it is very necessary for us to pick up some basic strength. We are not just careless, carefree people, but our attitude is one of having basic strength, basic energy.

47

Keep the three inseparable.

Your practice of lojong should be wholehearted and complete. In body, speech, and mind, you should be inseparable from lojong.

48

Train without bias in all areas.
It is crucial always to do this pervasively
and wholeheartedly.

The practice of lojong includes everyone and everything. It is important to be thorough and impartial in your practice, excluding nothing at all that comes up in your experience.

49

Always meditate on whatever provokes
resentment.

Always meditate on that which is most difficult. If you do not start right away, the moment difficulty arises, it is very hard to overcome it.

50

Don't be swayed by external circumstances.

Although your external circumstances may vary, your practice should not be dependent on that. Whether you are sick or well, rich or poor, have a good reputation or bad reputation, you should practice lojong. It is very simple: if your situation is right, breathe that out; if your situation is wrong, breathe that in.

51

This time, practice the main points.

"This time" refers to this lifetime. You have wasted many lives in the past, and in the future you may not have the opportunity to practice. But now, as a human being who has heard the dharma, you do. So without wasting any more time, you should practice the main points.

This teaching is threefold: [1] the benefit of others is more important than yourself, [2] practicing the teachings of the guru is more important than analytical study, [3] practicing bodhichitta is more important than any other practice.

52

Don't misinterpret.

There are six things that you may twist or misinterpret in your practice: patience, yearning, excitement, compassion, priorities, and joy. It is a misinterpretation of patience to be patient about everything in your life but the practice of dharma. Misinterpreted yearning is to foster yearning for pleasure and wealth but not to encourage the yearning to practice dharma thoroughly and properly. Misinterpreted excitement is to get excited by wealth and entertainment, but not to be excited by the study of dharma. It is twisted compassion to be compassionate to those who endure hardships in order to practice dharma, but to be unconcerned and uncompassionate to those who do evil. Twisted priorities means to work diligently out of self-interest at that which benefits you in the world, but not to practice dharma. Twisted joy is to be happy when sorrow afflicts your enemies, but not to rejoice in virtue and in the joy of transcending samsara. You should absolutely and completely stop all six of those misinterpretations.

53

Don't vacillate.

You should not vacillate in your enthusiasm for practice. If you sometimes practice and other times do not, that will not give birth to certainty in the dharma. Therefore, don't think too much. Just concentrate one-pointedly on mind training.

54

Train wholeheartedly.

Trust yourself and your practice wholeheartedly. Train purely in lojong—singlemindedly, with no distractions.

55

Liberate yourself by examining and analyzing.

Simply look at your mind and analyze it. By doing those two things, you should be liberated from kleshas and ego-clinging. Then you can practice lojong.

56

Don't wallow in self-pity.

Don't feel sorry for yourself. If somebody else achieves success or inherits a million dollars, don't waste time feeling bad because it wasn't you.

57

Don't be jealous.

If somebody else receives praise and you don't, don't be envious.

58

Don't be frivolous.

Don't demonstrate frivolous jealousy at your friends' success. If an acquaintance is wearing a new tie or a new blouse that you yourself would like, don't capriciously point out its shortcomings to him or her. "Yes, it's nice, but it has a stain on it." That will only serve to irritate him and won't help either his or your practice.

59

Don't expect applause.

Don't expect others to praise you or raise toasts to you. Don't count on receiving credit for your good deeds or good practice.

Concluding Verses

. .
.

When the five dark ages occur,
This is the way to transform them into the path of bodhi.
This is the essence of the amrita of the oral instructions,
Which were handed down from the tradition of the sage of
   Suvarnadvipa.

Having awakened the karma of previous training
And being urged on by intense dedication,
I disregarded misfortune and slander
And received oral instruction on taming ego-fixation.
Now, even at death, I will have no regrets.

[These two verses are the concluding comments of Geshe Chekawa
Yeshe Dorje, the author of *The Root Text of the Seven Points of Training the Mind.*]

APPENDIX: *Forty-six Ways in Which a Bodhisattva Fails*

• •
•

THIRTY-FOUR CONTRADICTIONS TO EMBODYING VIRTUE

CONTRADICTIONS TO THE PARAMITA OF GENEROSITY

Contradictions to Generosity with Regard to Material Things
1. Not offering to the three jewels
2. Giving in to possessiveness

Contradictions to the Generosity of Protection from Fear
3. Not respecting more experienced people
4. Not answering questions

Those That Prevent the Generosity of Others
5. Not accepting invitations as a guest
6. Angrily refusing gifts

Contradiction to Generosity with Regard to Dharma
7. Not teaching the dharma to those who want it

CONTRADICTIONS TO THE PARAMITA OF DISCIPLINE

Contradictions Mainly to Benefiting Others
1. Rejecting those who do not keep their discipline
2. Not developing learning, which inspires others' faith
3. Making little effort for the benefit of sentient beings

4. Not performing evil actions even though it is permitted when one has compassion and there is a need

Contradictions Mainly to Benefiting Oneself
5. Willingly taking up any of the five kinds of wrong livelihood
6. Mindlessly indulging
7. Due to desire and attachment, remaining in samsara

Contradictions to Benefiting Both Oneself and Others
8. Not preventing getting a bad reputation
9. Not controlling the kleshas

CONTRADICTIONS TO THE PARAMITA OF PATIENCE

1. Not practicing the four dharmas of a practitioner (not returning curses for curses, anger for anger, blow for blow, or insult for insult)
2. Not working peacefully with, but rejecting, people who are angry at you
3. Refusing to accept another's apology
4. Giving in to anger

CONTRADICTIONS TO THE PARAMITA OF EXERTION

1. Collecting followers for fame and fortune
2. Not overcoming laziness and so forth
3. Indulging in busyness and chatter

CONTRADICTIONS TO THE PARAMITA OF MEDITATION

1. Not seeking instruction in samadhi
2. Not abandoning obscurations to meditation
3. Viewing the experience of meditation as good and being attached to it

CONTRADICTIONS TO THE PARAMITA OF PRAJNA

Faults Related to Lesser Things
1. Not respecting the shravakayana, and therefore rejecting it
2. Having abandoned one's own tradition, the mahayana, exerting oneself in the shravakayana
3. In the same way, studying non-Buddhist literature

4. Although exerting oneself in the mahayana, preferring shravaka and non-Buddhist literature

Faults Related to Excellent Things

5. Not taking interest in the distinctive features of mahayana
6. Not seeking the holy dharma due to pride, laziness, and so forth
7. Praising oneself and disparaging others
8. Relying on the words rather than the meaning

TWELVE CONTRADICTIONS TO BENEFITING SENTIENT BEINGS

GENERAL APPLICATION

1. Not helping those in need
2. Not caring for the sick
3. Not removing the suffering of others
4. Not correcting those who are heedless

SPECIFIC APPLICATION

Faults of Not Being Helpful

1. Not repaying kindness
2. Not removing the pain of others
3. Not giving to those in need even though you can
4. Not benefiting those around you
5. Not acting in accord with the customs of others
6. Not praising those who have good qualities

Faults of Not Overpowering

1. Not overpowering those on a perverted path
2. Not taming with miracles and higher perceptions those who must be tamed in that way

[Translated by the Nālandā Translation Committee from the compilation of Jamgön Kongtrül the Great in his *Treasury of Knowledge*.]

Notes

••
•

Editor's Preface

1. The Kadam lineage, founded by Dromtönpa, the main disciple of Atisha, places great emphasis on monastic discipline, the cultivation of bodhichitta and compassion, and mind training. This emphasis was carried into the Kagyü lineage by Gampopa, who studied with Kadampa teachers prior to studying with Milarepa.

2. For further discussion of the origin and history of these teachings, see Geshe Kelsang Gyatso, *Universal Compassion*; Jamgön Kongtrül, *The Great Path of Awakening*; Geshe Rapten and Geshe Ngawang Dhargyey, *Advice from a Spiritual Friend*.

3. Vidyadhara: "insight or awareness holder" or "crazy-wisdom holder," an honorific title given to the author of this book, Chögyam Trungpa.

4. Vajradhatu is an association of Buddhist meditation centers founded by Chögyam Trungpa.

Introduction

1. *Hinayana, mahayana,* and *vayrayana* refer to the three stages of an individual's practice according to Tibetan Buddhism, not to the different schools of Buddhist practice. See Glossary.

Point Two

1. The word *not* is a conditional one, as it is usually linked with an object—not this or not that; the word *no* is unconditional: simply, No!

2. In vajrayana practice, students identify with the different styles of awakened energy by visualizing themselves as deities. These visualizations arise out of and dissolve back into emptiness.

3. The complete translation of these sayings reads:
    [1] May their evil deeds ripen in me.
    May all my virtue without exception ripen in them.

[2] I offer all my profit and gain to sentient beings, those honorable ones; I will take on all loss and defeat.

[3] May all the evil deeds and suffering of sentient beings ripen in me, and all my virtue and happiness ripen in sentient beings.

POINT THREE

1. "According to the traditional pattern of categorizing the three kayas, it is usually the other way around, that is, dharmakaya, sambhogakaya, and nirmanakaya."—Chögyam Trungpa.

2. The *Uttaratantra* is an important mahayana text on buddha nature transmitted by the bodhisattva Maitreya through the great teacher Asanga, and is one of his five treasuries.

3. The *Diamond Sutra* is a 300-line text, known in Sanskrit as the *Vajrachedika Prajnaparamita Sutra*, or the "perfection of wisdom that cuts like a diamond." It is one of the shorter and most well-known of the perfection of wisdom literature, the mahayana teachings on emptiness.

4. *Dikpa* means "evil deeds," or actions that lead one away from enlightenment. It often acts in partnership with *dripa*, or "obscurations." Dripa is divided into two classes, or veils: conflicting emotions and primitive beliefs about reality.

5. The Pön tradition is the native, pre-Buddhist religion of Tibet.

POINT FOUR

1. A traditional phrase expressive of the mahayana view that all sentient beings at one time or another have been our mothers and thus should be treated with the utmost love and respect.

2. The sevenfold service is a traditional mahayana liturgy consisting of seven steps: prostration, offering, confession, rejoicing in the virtue of others, requesting the teachers to teach, asking the teacher to remain and not pass into nirvana, and dedicating the merit of one's practice for the benefit of all sentient beings.

Glossary

• •
•

alaya: The fundamental unbiased ground of mind.

alaya-vijnana: Arising from the ground of alaya, alaya-vijnana, the eighth consciousness, is the point at which subtle seeds of bias or duality begin to appear. As such it is the root of samsara.

amrita: Blessed liquor, used in vajrayana meditation practices. More generally, spiritual intoxication. Also, profound essence of the teachings.

Avalokiteshvara: Bodhisattva of compassion.

bardo: "Existing in-between." Generally used to refer to the intermediate state after death and before the next rebirth. [Also spelled *pardo*.]

basic goodness: Unconditional goodness of mind at its most basic level. The natural goodness of alaya.

bodhi: "Awake." The path of bodhi is a means of awakening from confusion.

bodhichitta: "Awakened mind/heart." Ultimate or absolute bodhichitta is the union of emptiness and compassion, the essential nature of awakened mind. Relative bodhichitta is the tenderness arising from a glimpse of ultimate bodhichitta that inspires one to train oneself to work for the benefit of others.

bodhisattva: "Awake being." A bodhisattva is someone who has completely overcome confusion and dedicated his or her life and all his or her actions to awakening or liberating all sentient beings.

bodhisattva path: Another term for the mahayana.

bodhisattva vow: The formal vow taken to mark one's aspiration to become a bodhisattva and one's actual entering the bodhisattva path of dedicating one's life to all sentient beings.

buddhadharma: See dharma.

dark ages (five): The five dark ages are (1) when life becomes shorter, (2) when the view is based on corruption of the teachings, (3) when kleshas become more solid, (4) when sentient beings become untameable and difficult to convert to the dharma, and (5) when it becomes a time of sickness, famine, and war.

dharma: 1. Teachings or truth, specifically the teachings of the Buddha, also called buddhadharma. 2. Phenomena in general.

dharmakaya: "Dharma-body." Basic unbounded openness of mind, wisdom beyond reference point. *See also* kaya.

dharmapala: "Dharma protector." A sudden reminder that shocks the confused practitioner awake. The dharmapalas represent basic awareness, which brings the confused practitioner back to his or her discipline.

dön: A sudden attack of neurosis that seems to come from outside oneself.

dorje: A ritual scepter, symbolizing skillful means [upaya], the masculine principle, which is used in tantric practice along with the bell, symbolizing knowledge [prajna], or the feminine principle. Together, bell and dorje symbolize the inseparability of masculine and feminine, skillful means and knowledge.

Gampopa (1079–1153): The fifth major Kagyü enlightened lineage holder and foremost disciple of the yogin Milarepa. Gampopa combined the Kadam teachings of Atisha with the mahamudra tradition stemming from the Indian masters Tilopa and Naropa.

Geluk: One of the four great lineages of Tibetan Buddhism, known as the reform tradition and emphasizing intellectual study and analysis.

hinayana: "Narrow way." The first of the three yanas of Tibetan Buddhism. The focus of the hinayana is on individual salvation through taming one's mind and on causing no harm to others. It is the essential starting point on the path.

Jamgön Kongtrül of Sechen (1901?–1960): Chögyam Trungpa's root teacher, one of the five incarnations of Jamgön Kongtrül the Great. "A big jolly man, friendly to all without distinction of rank, very generous and with a great sense of humor combined with deep understanding; he was always sympathetic to the troubles of others."—Chögyam Trungpa.

Jamgön Kongtrül the Great (1813–1899): One of the principal teachers of nineteenth-century Tibet, the author of the commentary on slogan practice entitled *The Basic Path Toward Enlightenment.* Jamgön Kongtrül was a leader in the religious reform movement called ri-me that sought to discourage sectarianism and encourage meditation practice and the application of Buddhist principles in everyday life.

jinpa: Generosity. One of the six paramitas.

Kadam: The Kadam lineage was founded by Dromtönpa, the main disciple of Atisha, who came to Tibet in the eleventh century. Their teachings place emphasis on monastic discipline and on training one's mind in bodhichitta and compassion.

Kagyü: One of the four great lineages of Tibetan Buddhism. The Kagyü lineage is known as the "Practice Lineage" because of its emphasis on meditative discipline.

kalyanamitra: "Spiritual friend." It is said that in the hinayana one views one's teacher as an elder, in the mahayana as a spiritual friend, and in the vajrayana as a vajra master.

karma: "Action." The entrapment of karma refers to the fact that our actions, since they are based on ego-clinging, entrap us in a never-ending chain of cause and effect from which it is more and more difficult to escape.

karuna: "Compassion."

kaya: Literally, "body." The four kayas refer in this text to four aspects of perception. Dharmakaya is the sense of openness; nirmanakaya is clarity; sambhogakaya is the link or relationship between those two; and svabhavikakaya is the total experience of the whole thing.

klesha: Mental poison, confused emotionality. The five root kleshas are passion or grasping, aggression, delusion or ignorance, arrogance, and envy

lojong: "Mind training." Specifically, the practice of cultivating bodhichitta outlined by the Kadampa slogans.

lord of speech: One of the three lords of materialism (lord of body, lord of speech, lord of mind), or ways in which we consume our physical, psychological, and spiritual experiences for the further bloating of ego's realm.

mahakala: A wrathful dharmapala, or dharma protector. Iconographically, mahakalas are depicted as dark and wrathful deities.

mahamudra: Literally, "great symbol." The central meditative transmission of the Kagyü lineage. The inherent clarity and wakefulness of mind, which is both vivid and empty.

mahayana: The "giant vehicle," which emphasizes the emptiness (shunyata) of all phenomena, compassion, and the acknowledgment of universal buddha nature. The ideal figure of the mahayana is the bodhisattva; hence it is often referred to as the bodhisattva path.

maitri: "Loving-kindness," "friendliness." In connection with compassion, or karuna, maitri refers to the process of making friends with oneself as the starting point for developing compassion for others.

maitri bhavana: The practice of maitri, or loving-kindness. Tonglen practice is also referred to as maitri practice, or maitri bhavana. This term also applies to a monthly practice for the sick conducted at Vajradhatu centers.

Manjushri: Bodhisattva of knowledge and learning. Usually depicted with a book and the sword of prajna.

Marpa (1012–1097): The third of the great Kagyü lineage holders and chief disciple of Naropa. Known as Marpa the translator, Marpa was the first Tibetan in this lineage and introduced many important teachings from India into Tibet.

Milarepa (1040–1123): The most famous of all Tibetan poets and quintessential wandering yogin, Milarepa, or the "cotton-clad Mila," was Marpa's chief student and the fourth major lineage holder of the Kagyü tradition.

mother sentient beings: A traditional phrase expressive of the view that all sentient beings, or living creatures, have at one time or another been one's mother.

nirmanakaya: "Emanation body," "form-body," or "body of manifestation." Communication of awakened mind through form—specifically, through embodiment as a human being. *See also* kaya.

nyingje: "Compassion." Literally, "noble heart." Tibetan translation for the Sanskrit *karuna.*

pak-yang: Carefree, relaxed mind. Positive naiveté. Trust in basic goodness.

paramita: Literally, "gone to the other shore." The essential activities of a bodhisattva, or enlightened being. The six paramitas are generosity, discipline, patience, exertion, meditation, and knowledge (prajna). The paramitas are called "transcendent actions" because they are nondual, not based on ego-clinging. Therefore, they transcend the entanglements of karma.

prajna: "Transcendent knowledge," the sixth paramita. Prajna is the eyes and the other five paramitas are the limbs of bodhisattva activity.

sadhana: A ritual text, as well as the accompanying practice. Ranging from very simple to more elaborate versions, sadhanas engage the mind through meditation, the body through gestures (*mudras*), and the speech through mantra recitation.

samaya: "Sacred word" or "vow." The vajrayana principle of commitment, whereby the student is bound completely to the discipline and to the teacher and to his or her own sanity.

sambhogakaya: "Body of enjoyment" or energy. The environment of compassion and communication linking the dharmakaya and the nirmanakaya. *See also* kaya.

sampannakrama: One of the two stages of vajrayana sadhana practice. Having dissolved the visualization (utpattikrama), one rests effortlessly in sampannakrama, or the completion stage of formless meditation.

samsara: The vicious cycle of existence, arising from ignorance and characterized by suffering.

sangha: The third of the three objects of refuge (Buddha, dharma, sangha). In a narrow sense sangha refers to Buddhist monks and nuns, in the mahayana sense, sangha refers to the entire body of practitioners, both lay and monastic.

self-liberate: Self-liberated means freed by itself, on the spot. In the slogan "Self-liberate even the antidote," the sense is that emptiness is free from solidification.

shamatha: Mindfulness practice. A basic meditation practice common to most schools of Buddhism, the aim of which is to tame the mind.

Shambhala: "The Shambhala teachings are founded on the premise that there is basic human wisdom that can help to solve the world's problems. This wisdom does not belong to any one culture or religion, nor does it come only from the West or the East. Rather it is a tradition of human warriorship that has existed in many cultures throughout history."—Chögyam Trungpa

shravakayana: "Way of the hearers." The focus of the shravakayana is on individual salvation through listening to the teachings and gaining insight into the four noble truths and the irreality of phenomena. The shravakayana can be equated with the hinayana.

shunyata: "Emptiness," "openness." A completely open and unbounded clarity of mind.

sugatagarbha: Indestructible basic wakefulness, buddha nature, similar to tathagatagarbha. *See also* tathagatagarbha.

Suvarnadvipa (sage of Suvarnadvipa): Atisha's teacher Dharmakirti lived on the island of Sumatra, in Sanskrit named Suvarnadvipa or the "golden island." Hence he was called the sage of Suvarnadvipa. In Tibetan, Dharmakirti was referred to as Serlingpa, "the man from Ser ling" (Tibetan for "golden land").

svabhavikakaya: "Body of self-nature." Total panoramic experience, the totality of the kayas. *See also* kaya

tantra: A synonym for vajrayana, the third of the three yanas of Tibetan Buddhism. *Tantra* means continuity and refers both to the root texts of the vajrayana and to the systems of meditation they describe.

tathagatagarbha: Buddha nature, the enlightened basic nature of all beings. *Tathagata* is an epithet of the Buddha, and *garbha* means "womb," or "essence."

tonglen: The practice of sending and taking, which is designed to reverse ego-clinging and cultivate bodhichitta.

utpattikrama: Visualization practice. One of the two stages of vajrayana sadhana practice in which one evokes awakened mind by visualizing a particular tantric deity.

vajrayana: "Indestructible vehicle or way." The third of the three yanas of Tibetan Buddhism.

vidyadhara: Insight holder or "crazy-wisdom holder." With a capital V, an honorific title given to Chögyam Trungpa.

vipashyana: Awareness practice. With shamatha, one of the two main modes of meditation common to most forms of Buddhism.

yana: "Vehicle." A coherent body of intellectual teachings and practical meditative methods related to a particular stage of a student's progress on the path of buddhadharma. The three main vehicles are the hinayana, mahayana, and vajrayana.

Transliterations of Tibetan Names and Terms

∴

Changchup Shunglam	*byang chub gzhung lam*
Chögyam Trungpa Rinpoche	*chos rgyam drung pa rin po che*
dathün	*zla thun*
dikpa	*sdig pa*
dön	*gdon*
Dromtönpa	*'brom ston pa*
Gampopa	*sgam po pa*
Geshe Chekawa Yeshe Dorje	*dge bshes 'chad ka ba ye shes rdo rje*
Jamgön Kongtrül	*'jam mgon kong sprul*
jinpa	*sbyin pa*
jukpa	*'jug pa*
Kadam(pa)	*bka' gdams pa*
Kagyü	*bka' brgyud*
kündzop	*kun rdzob*
lamkhyer	*lam khyer*
Lang-ri Thangpa	*glang ri thang pa*
lojong	*blo sbyong*
Marpa	*mar pa*
Milarepa	*mi la ras pa*
mönpa	*smon pa*
nyingje	*snying rje*
nyön-yid	*nyon yid*
nyönmong	*nyon mongs*
pak-yang	*bag yangs*
pö shung	*bod gzhung*

pön	*bon*
Samye Ling	*bsam yas gling*
Serlingpa	*gser gling pa*
Surmang	*zur mang*
tonglen	*gtong len*
torma	*gtor ma*
tsültim	*tshul khrims*
yi	*yid*

Bibliography

••
•

Chattopadhyaya, Aloka. *Atisha and Tibet*. Calcutta: R. D. Press, 1967.

Chödrön, Pema. *Start Where You Are: A Guide to Compassionate Living*. Boston: Shambhala, 1994.

Gyatso, Geshe Kelsang. *Universal Compassion*. London: Tharpa Publishing, 1988.

Gyatso, Tenzin (H.H. the Fourteenth Dalai Lama). *Kindness, Clarity, and Insight*. Ithaca, N.Y.: Snow Lion Publications, 1984.

Kelsang, Lama Thubten, et al. *Atisha*. Bangkok: Social Science Association Press of Thailand, 1974. Reprinted, Delhi: Mahayana Publications, 1983.

Kongtrül, Jamgön. *The Great Path of Awakening*. Translated by Ken McLeod. Boston and London: Shambhala Publications, 1987.

Rapten, Geshe, and Dhargyey, Geshe Ngawang. *Advice from a Spiritual Friend*. Edited by Brian Beresford. New Delhi: Publications for Wisdom Culture, 1977. Revised edition, London: Wisdom Publications, 1984.

Tai Situ, Khentin. *Way to Go*. Edited by Ken Holmes. Eskdalemuir, Scotland: Kagyu Samye Ling.

Wallace, B. Alan. *A Passage from Solitude: Training the Mind in a Life Embracing the World*. Edited by Zara Houshmand. Ithaca, N.Y.: Snow Lion Publications, 1992.

About the Slogan Cards

· ·
·

Cards printed with each of the Kadam slogans for use in one's practice of mind training are available for purchase from the following book-stores:

Vajradhatu Publications
1678 Barrington
Halifax, Nova Scotia
Canada B3J 2A2
(902) 421-1550

Samadhi Store
30 Church Street
Barnet, VT 05821
(800) 331-7751
Web site: *www.samadhicushions.com*

Ziji
9148 Kerry Road
Boulder, CO 80303
(800) 565-8470
Web site: *www.ziji.com*

About the Author

• •
•

Ven. Chögyam Trungpa was born in the province of Kham in Eastern Tibet in 1939. When he was just thirteen months old, Chögyam Trungpa was recognized as a major *tülku* or incarnate teacher. According to Tibetan tradition, an enlightened teacher is capable, based on his or her vow of compassion, of reincarnating in human form over a succession of generations. Before dying, such a teacher might leave a letter or other clues to the whereabouts of the next incarnation. Later, students and other realized teachers look through these clues and, based on careful examination of dreams and visions, conduct searches to discover and recognize the successor. Thus, particular lines of teaching are formed, in some cases extending over several centuries. Chögyam Trungpa was the eleventh in the teaching lineage known as the Trungpa tülkus.

Once young tülkus are recognized, they enter a period of intensive training in the theory and practice of the Buddhist teachings. Trungpa Rinpoche (*Rinpoche* is an honorific title meaning "precious one"), after being enthroned as supreme abbot of Surmang monasteries and governor of Surmang District, began a period of training that would last eighteen years, until his departure from Tibet in 1959. As a Kagyü tülku, his training was based on the systematic practice of meditation and on refined theoretical understanding of Buddhist philosophy. One of the four great lineages of Tibet, the Kagyü is known as the Practice Lineage.

At the age of eight, Trungpa Rinpoche received ordination as a novice monk. After his ordination, he engaged in intensive study and practice of the traditional monastic disciplines as well as in the arts of calligraphy, thangka painting, and monastic dance. His primary teachers were Jamgön Kongtrül of Sechen and Khenpo Kangshar—leading teachers in the Nyingma and Kagyü lineages. In 1958, at the age of eighteen, Trungpa Rinpoche completed his studies, receiving the degrees of *kyorpön* (doctor of divinity) and *khenpo* (master of studies). He also received full monastic ordination.

The late fifties were a time of great upheaval in Tibet. As it became clear that the Chinese Communists intended to take over the country by force, many people, both monastic and lay, fled the country. Trungpa Rinpoche spent many harrowing months trekking over the Himalayas (described in his book *Born in Tibet*). After narrowly escaping capture by the Chinese, he at last reached India in 1959. While in India, Trungpa Rinpoche was appointed to serve as spiritual adviser to the Young Lamas Home School in Dalhousie, India. He served in this capacity from 1959 to 1963.

Trungpa Rinpoche's first opportunity to encounter the West came when he received a Spaulding sponsorship to attend Oxford University. At Oxford he studied comparative religion, philosophy, and fine arts. He also studied Japanese flower arranging, receiving a degree from the Sogetsu School. While in England, Trungpa Rinpoche began to instruct Western students in the dharma (the teachings of the Buddha), and in 1968 he cofounded the Samye Ling Meditation Centre in Dumfriesshire, Scotland. During this period he also published his first two books in English: *Born in Tibet* and *Meditation in Action*.

In 1969, Trungpa Rinpoche traveled to Bhutan, where he entered into a solitary meditation retreat. This retreat marked a pivotal change in his approach to teaching. Immediately upon returning he became a lay person, putting aside his monastic robes and dressing in ordinary Western attire. He also married a young Englishwoman, and together they left Scotland and moved to North America. Many of his early students found these changes shocking and upsetting. However, he expressed a conviction that, in order to take root in the West, the dharma needed to be taught free from cultural trappings and religious fascination.

During the seventies America was in a period of political and cultural ferment. It was a time of fascination with the East. Trungpa Rinpoche criticized the materialistic and commercialized approach to spirituality he encountered, describing it as a "spiritual supermarket." In his lectures, and in his books *Cutting Through Spiritual Materialism* and *The Myth of Freedom*, he pointed to the simplicity and directness of the practice of sitting meditation as the way to cut through such distortions of the spiritual journey.

During his seventeen years of teaching in North America, Trungpa Rinpoche developed a reputation as a dynamic and controversial teacher. Fluent in the English language, he was one of the first lamas who could speak to Western students directly, without the aid of a translator. Traveling extensively throughout North America and Europe, Trungpa Rinpoche gave hundreds of talks and seminars. He established major centers in Vermont, Colorado, and Nova Scotia, as well as many smaller meditation and study centers in cities throughout North America and Europe. Vajradhatu was formed in 1973 as the central administrative body of this network.

In 1974, Trungpa Rinpoche founded the Naropa Institute, which became the only accredited Buddhist-inspired university in North America. He lectured extensively at the Institute, and his book *Journey without Goal* is based on a course he taught there. In 1976, he established the Shambhala Training program, a series of weekend programs and seminars that provides instruction in meditation practice within a secular setting. His book *Shambhala: The Sacred Path of the Warrior* gives an overview of the Shambhala teachings.

In 1976, Trungpa Rinpoche appointed Ösel Tendzin (Thomas F. Rich) as his Vajra Regent, or dharma heir. Ösel Tendzin worked closedly with Trungpa Rinpoche in the administration of Vajradhatu and Shambhala Training. He taught extensively from 1976 until his death in 1990 and is the author of *Buddha in the Palm of Your Hand*.

Trungpa Rinpoche was also active in the field of translation. Working with Francesca Fremantle, he rendered a new translation of *The Tibetan Book of the Dead*, which was published in 1975. Later he formed the Nālandā Translation Committee, in order to translate texts and liturgies for his own students as well as to make important texts available publicly.

In 1979, Trungpa Rinpoche conducted a ceremony empowering his son Ösel Rangdröl Mukpo as his successor in the Shambhala lineage. In 1995, His Holiness Penor Rinpoche, supreme head of the Nyingma lineage, enthroned him as *Sakyong*, "earth protector." He is now known as Sakyong Mipham Rinpoche.

Index

•••